THE LIFE AND TIMES

OF

ARTHUR HENRY

A.H. CREIGHTON

BLACKWATER PRESS

Printed in Ireland at the press of the publishers

© 1994 Blackwater Press,
Broomhill Road,
Tallaght,
Dublin 24.

ISBN   0 86 121 5931

Editor
Anna O'Donovan

Layout
Edward Callan

Front Cover
Philip Ryan

CONTENTS

ACKNOWLEDGEMENTS

This book is dedicated to, first, my wife Gladys and, second, the company which I served all my business life – Musgrave Ltd. Without the support of one, my success with the other would not have been possible and this book would never have been written.

My sincere thanks to Shirley Mills who typed every word, bit by bit, over several years; to Norma O'Sullivan and her husband Dominic, Nancy Motherway, Mary Hoare and Helen Ross – and to the countless others who provided leads and information without any knowledge of how useful these were to my endeavours.

Whilst all the characters depicted are real, some, unfortunately, are no longer with us and in other cases not all the names of people or places are the original ones – this is to save anyone from any possible embarrassment.

An abridged version of my account of Roches Point appeared in *The Cork Hollybough* in the Christmas 1991 issue.

A.H. Creighton

INTRODUCTION

I joined Musgrave Brothers (now Musgrave Limited) in 1927 and spent all my working life, 50 years, with the company, retiring from the position of Marketing Director in 1977.

I was selected to introduce the system known as Voluntary Group Trading in 1960, leading on to today's chain of independent retailers under the SuperValue-Centra symbols.

This book is about my career during those years and incorporates a large part of my family history as well.

When I retired I undertook the editing and production of the company magazine, *Musgrave News,* for eight years and I have had articles accepted in *Choice* magazine (England) and *The Cork Hollybough*.

Book 1
Early Days

CHAPTER 1

STARTING OUT

I was born on 29 July 1912 in the city of Cork in Southern Ireland, the last in a family of five. I could never figure out how my parents managed it, but there was two years between my only sister Emily and my eldest brother Charles – three years between him and Albert – four between Albert and William and five between William and me.

I remember hearing something about being an "after-thought" but I had no idea what that meant, so it didn't trouble me. I went to Christchurch National School, situated near the Church of the same name, and now since demolished. We lived on the Boreenmanna Road and walked to school, about two miles, in all weathers. I well remember my first day at school as I caused an uproar when I wouldn't be separated from my brother Bill. He had to use his most persuasive manner to get me to go to the infants class. I also remember, but with very different feelings, one fateful morning twelve months later when I was sitting on the rung of the kitchen table trying to tie my boot laces. The lace broke and I shouted in my child's treble " F--- it". The chatter in the kitchen stopped dead and in the deafening silence a strong hand hauled me out by the scruff of the neck and delivered a resounding smack to the side of my head. "Where did you hear that word ?" my father asked while shaking me like a dog would shake a rat. I knew full well where I had heard it and so did my big brother, but I knew I couldn't tell. So, after another smack I was released and we rushed out of the house as quick as we could.

Plodding down the road, Bill and I looked at each other and then started laughing. "Thanks Arthur," he said, "I was afraid I was in for it too." "What does it mean anyway ?" I asked. "You'll find out soon enough," he answered and that was all I could discover. I can also remember going into the city with my mother and shopping in the meat market, which hasn't changed much over the years, and also at Musgrave Brothers, where my father worked and where we got our ration of tea and sugar as World War I was in full swing.

Situated at 84 Grand Parade, demolished on the construction of The Queens Old Castle Shopping Centre, Musgrave Brothers was a tall narrow building running almost the full length of Brunswick Street, behind the present St Augustine's Church. There was a retail shop on the Grand Parade and the remainder of the premises was for wholesale groceries and general business. The facia bore the name "Musgrave Brothers Limited", and under that "Expert Tea Blenders", cut in timber and embellished in gold paint, faced with glass. One shop window was half blacked out and then topped with a gold band and inscribed, also in gold, with the legend "Wholesale and Retail Grocers". This was quite a common shop front then.

The other window usually had an artistically arranged display of tea; there were no special offers and nothing was priced. Inside, a long mahogany counter ran the full length of the shop. The walls were a series of drawers with labels stating the contents, such as pearl barley, caraway seeds and rice, and shelves for tins, glass jars and sweets in bottles. At the end of the counter, where the top had been removed, a large bin had been created to hold sugar. There was no pre-packaging and, except for tins and a very limited range of canned goods and bottles, all goods had to be weighed and bagged. In front of the counter was an array of square tins, approximately nine inches by ten inches deep with hinged glass tops, all containing loose biscuits. I think the reason I remember all this so well was because my Uncle, Jim Hazlett – who was the Charge Hand – never failed to give me a biscuit or two and better still, he allowed me to choose. My cousin, Annie Hazlett, also worked there. She was Mr Stuart Musgrave's secretary. We heard an awful lot about Musgraves in our house from my father, he was Head Book-Keeper and was responsible for the payment of all accounts and the pricing of invoices. He occupied an office on the second floor.

The wholesale entrance was in Brunswick Street and on the first floor was what was known as "The Fancy Room". Besides carrying all sweet confectionery, it stocked toiletries and a considerable range of non-grocery items, like household hardware, brushware, toys, wicker baskets, clocks, haberdashery, stationery, paints, padlocks, penknives, medicines (Beechams Pills, iodine, Friars Balsam), and ointments (boracic, zinc and Vaseline to name a few). Many unusual items were also sold, such as boot protectors and studs, breakfast cans, busks (corsets!), horse clippers, carbide (for acetylene lamps), cobblers' wax, collar supports, garters, garter and hat elastic, flower pot covers, hemp, lamp wick, liquorice powders and melodians. And also all kinds of needles, smoking pipes, rubber heels and soles, skipping ropes, watches, washboards, not to mention scapulars, rosary beads and prayer books. All were important as the local shop had to supply anything and everything, particularly in the country areas where a visit to town by horse and cart was not an everyday event.

The Grocery Department also carried many products now long forgotten such as alum, axle grease, butter colouring, black lead, butter preservative, camomile flowers, cascara, curried rabbit, camphor, copperas (for potato spray), Epsom Salts which were a big seller for both cattle and humans. Essence of rennet (used in butter-making), hat dyes, lemonade crystals and powders, linseed meal, pistachio kernels, insect powder, Seidlitz Powders, Scotts Emulsion, vermin paste, waterglass (for preserving eggs), and the famous cure-all ointment, Zam Buk, were also available. The most important item however was carried on the top floor – known as the Tea Loft. It is very interesting to quote from a very early travellers' advice booklet, measuring only three and a half inches by two and a half inches, as follows:

BLENDED TEAS

We have confidence in directing special attention to this most important branch of our business, which we have studied with the greatest care in all its details, and our long experience enables us to select and blend teas that we can recommend with confidence.

The steady growth of our tea trade is very satisfactory proof of the value which we offer and it is very pleasing to find that our Customers appreciate our efforts to supply blends suitable for their trade and district, and we shall be pleased to submit samples on receipt of enquiry.

If we expended large sums of money on advertising, like firms in the trade are in the habit of doing, then the satisfactory increase in this branch of our business would not be so remarkable. But we believe that our customers have always been our best advertisers, and therefore we consider it much more advisable to supply them with teas at the Lowest Possible Price without having to make them pay additional expenses caused by such advertising.

ORIGINAL TEAS

To buyers of Original Teas we always have pleasure in submitting samples from our carefully chosen stocks of the growths of India, Ceylon, Java, etc., which we can offer "in-bond" or "duty paid" (original packages).

We take the opportunity to thank our many friends in all parts of Ireland for the continued favours during the past year and to assure them that it will always be our desire to supply such value in all branches of our business as will merit a continuance of those favours during the coming years.

Musgrave Brothers Limited

What an interesting window into business thinking in 1916-1917! All teas were sold in bulk, 100lb chests or 50lb half chests, and there were many blends on offer –"Specially blended to suit the local water," was a common selling phrase.

We heard many stories from my father of "Number 84" and the Boss, John Laird Musgrave, Such as how one day "Johnny" – as the staff nick-named him amongst themselves – was on one of his usual routine rounds of the departments. While descending quietly in the lift, he spotted a man with his arms hanging by his sides gazing out of the window at the street scene below. John L., who wore rubber heels, silently walked up behind him and the man nearly jumped out of his skin when he heard the voice, "Well Murphy, what are you doing here?" Caught unawares, Murphy blurted out, "Nothing Mr John," and fled. John continued on to the next loft where he came upon another worker and when asked what he was doing, he replied, "Helping Murphy, Sir."

There was another genius working there who had a crazy idea that he wanted to be a film actor. One day while carrying a big stack of boxes of confectionery, he imagined he was acting like a famous actor, and walked straight into a glass door and split the glass from top to bottom. He didn't lose his job but two shilling and six pence was deducted from his pay every week until the cost of replacement was met!

The staff also played pranks on each other. On one occasion there was a woman-crazy member of the staff – he was always making dates, often from the advertisements which commonly appeared in the paper in those days, e.g. "nice girl would like to meet nice gentleman," etc. So the staff put a similar advertisement in the paper to tempt him and, low and behold, he replied.

They wrote back to him and asked him to keep an appointment to meet the lady concerned – where else but across the road from 84 Grand Parade! In due time, the poor chap was standing on the pavement anxiously looking up and down and, needless to say, the bright boys and girls in "84" were looking out the window waiting until he got fed up. One of the girls went over and said, "Well, here I am". He didn't know what to say and you could hear the laughter all over the house.

Musgrave – A seed is sown

Little did I think that one day I too would be working for Musgrave Brothers. Indeed, I was to spend my whole life with the same Company. But where did the business originate? The first Musgrave shop was set up in 1876 as a retail grocery shop operating in North Main Street, Cork. It was owned by Thomas and Stuart Musgrave who were natives of Co. Leitrim. It is not known what brought them to Cork but it turned out to be a very good time to start a grocery business.

The Land Acts of 1881 and similar Acts in 1891 and 1903 made it possible for farmers to own their own land. Previously, they had only been tenants without rights. The results of this began to show because at that time business was good. By 1887 the two brothers decided to move their business to 84 Grand Parade and in 1893 also started a shop in Denny Street, Tralee, Co. Kerry. In 1894 that partnership was dissolved and Musgrave Brothers Limited was formed.

The new company promptly embarked on the development of a substantial property in King Street (now known as MacCurtain Street) and in 1895 they opened a sweet factory and decided to build a hotel and shops – one of which they would operate themselves. Also in the early 1890s, the Company got involved in the Laundry business, calling it the Metropole Laundry. The hotel was called the Metropole Hotel. They also had a coal distribution business, Metropole Coal.

The railway brought newly prosperous country people into the city and, at the station, one of the Musgrave staff would distribute a hand bill inviting them to visit their shops. They were a very progressive company.

Cork, at the turn of the century, was a prosperous city with a population of approximately 95,000 people sprawling across an island between the north and south channels of the River Lee and climbing up the adjoining hills. In its earlier days it was called "The Venice of the North" because it consisted of numerous islands and canals. The main canal linked the north and south channels, this was covered over and became the main thoroughfare, Patrick's Street. If you stand on Patrick's Bridge and look down river, you can see the entrance to the canal on your right, stand over on the south channel at Sullivan's Quay and you will see where it emerged on the opposite bank. Patrick's Street was paved with oak blocks then but when a high tide combined with a strong wind, too much water was forced into the canal and would burst up through the paving. That was time for many poor people to descend with box-carts and carry off as many blocks as possible before the police caught them. They made great kindling.

A light electric tram-way system ran from St Luke's Cross on the northern heights along King Street and over Patrick's Bridge to the Father Matthew statue, and from there to Douglas. Another line ran from the statue to Blackpool on the lower north side.

The statue was that of Father Theobald Matthew, the Apostle of Temperance, who was born in Cork in 1790. The main railway station was on the flatland beneath St Luke's and Montenotte – where the gentry lived. The station had nationwide connections to Tralee, Limerick, Dublin and Wexford and all points in between; lines also ran to Galway in the west, and to Belfast. There were three other railways operating, the Bandon and Southcoast, the Passage and Crosshaven line, and the Muskerry Tram. As the Muskerry tram ran alongside the roads and across country, rumours circulated about an unwritten rule – "Blackberry picking is forbidden while the train is in motion".

There was also a prosperous brewery and a distillery business, giving much employment. There was a ship-building yard at Passage, and Cork was a very busy port. Some of the old business names are still operating, apart from Musgrave Brothers (now Musgrave Ltd), a few others are still going strong. These include: Murphy's Brewery which is now owned by Heineken, a Dutch company; Cork Distillers, later absorbed into Irish Distillers owned by the French company Pernod Ricard; Roches Stores, then known as "The London House", and also Cash & Co.

My Dad and Me

By 1920 Musgrave Brothers was due for another expansion. The Board, under the chairmanship of John L. Musgrave (his father, Thomas, had died in 1917), decided to build a new warehouse in Cornmarket Street. Previously they had considered building on a site bounded by Liberty Street, Cross Street, Washington Street and North Main Street, but when they failed to purchase all of the houses required Cornmarket Street became the target.

In 1921, my mother passed away and my sister became "the woman of the house". This brought my father and me very much closer and we spent more time together at the weekends. We followed hurling, being ardent supporters of Blackrock (never known by any other name but "The Rockies") even though my father was born in Kilkenny. "I am a Kilkenny cat," he would say, "with nine lives and none of them gone yet." When Kilkenny met Cork in the hurling he would say, "Well, if Cork are winning I will cheer for them and if Kilkenny are winning I will give them my shout."

A favourite walk on Sundays was to take the Crosshaven train to Rochestown, where we had lemonade and cakes at Ford's Café. Then we would walk the three miles to Douglas and take a tram home. We also went coursing with Blackrock Coursing Club near Lakelands. We had to get special permission from the Pike family to course over their grounds at Bessboro. Their house is now a Convent and the lands have all been built on.

My father had some great sayings and used them well. When we boys were squabbling he would say, "Stop fighting lads, you are only alive a few years and will be dead and forgotten for thousands." He was a heavy pipe smoker and kept two pipes going, as one burnt down he would light another. When my brother started smoking cigarettes, he said to me, "Never smoke and you'll never want to". He was a generous man who found it hard to say No and who firmly believed that a man's word was his bond, so he didn't lie. Therefore, he had a problem when persistent so-called "friends" would request a fill of tobacco too frequently! He solved this problem by getting a second pouch which he called "All The World", he kept this one empty. When asked for a fill that he felt was an imposition he would say, "Sorry old chap but I haven't a bit in All The World". He was widely known by all creeds and classes and a very popular figure. I never heard him insulting anyone and if he heard anyone else doing so, he would say, "Look, if you haven't anything good to say, say nothing at all".

At that time, a whole new world was about to open up for me. I was nine years old and worked hard at school – my best subjects were English and Mathematics. I can well remember one day when our class was engaged in a mental arithmetic exercise. Up to then I was somewhat slow at this – though good on paper – but that day I was suddenly aware that if I concentrated I could "see" the figures mentally, and from then on it all became easier.

One day my father came home from work and said to my sister, "Well, Emily, John L. has bought some property in Roches Point. There is a house where senior staff can stay free of charge for the fortnight's annual holidays."

Again John L. proved himself ahead in his thinking for staff welfare was not in the minds of most bosses at all.

CHAPTER 2

ROCHES POINT

R oches Point is a promontory on which there is a lighthouse at the mouth of Cork's beautiful harbour, one of the finest in the world. Leading to the lighthouse gates there was a row of houses, nestling under the rocks and facing the harbour. There was a boathouse and slipway backed by a triangular green beyond which lay the coastguard station with large gardens running from each house to the sea and all neatly enclosed by a low wall.

We did not hesitate in deciding to go. For me, going to the Point was the highlight of the year, and what a journey it seemed then! For weeks preceding our departure there were feverish preparations and mounting excitement. Finally, the great day arrived; puffing and wheezing, the Ford car and driver hired to take us there pulled up at our door and the big job of loading began. Besides my sister, my brothers, and my father, there was a huge array of groceries, cans of meat, biscuits and sweets, bundles of clothes to wear and for beds, fishing rods, nets, gaffs and toy sailing ships, not to mention the dog and the cat!

These Ford cars were not the covered saloons known today but had a hood that folded down at the back and if it happened to rain we had some job to get it all pulled up and the side screens fitted. Even then you did not remain dry for long.

It usually took several hours to travel the 29 miles of very uneven road. Once we lost our dog, and we concluded that she must have fallen off past Midleton, a town 12 miles from Cork city. We didn't expect to see her again, but lo and behold, she arrived back at our home in Cork about ten days later. She was bedraggled and thin but none the worse from her long walk. During the times of the "troubles" we carried a few stout planks which enabled us to negotiate the trenches cut in the roads where the British forces were stopped and ambushed. There was also plenty of other excitement, when my father smoked his pipe – with the wind blowing and hood down, he set us on fire at least twice. But it didn't stop him smoking!

The house to be our holiday home was the last in the row of houses leading to the lighthouse, and there was one building beyond and we also had the use of that. Judging by the pointed windows, it was once a place of worship of some sort, but we found it a great place to play handball on wet days. The Coastguard Station was operated by a Head Coastguard who lived in the middle house. His two assistants each had a large house at either end, and the other six or eight houses were occupied by the lower ranking coastguards. The gaunt tower, still standing on the high ground behind our terrace of houses, was then a very busy place. It had a tall pole protruding from its centre, on which were mounted large signalling arms and there was an outside iron platform running around the tower. Here, the Coastguards manned the watch, ship fashion, 24 hours a day. You could tell the time as their footsteps clattered along the road between the Coastguard Station and the tower every four hours. The arms were used to signal incoming ships using the method called semaphore whereby the different positions of the arms indicated different letters of the alphabet. This was the only means of communicating with the ships then, regarding piloting arrangements etc., as radio was only in its infancy. There was much more shipping then, ships were smaller and there were more of them. We also had the transatlantic liners travelling between Queenstown, as Cobh was then called, and New York, on a regular basis.

There was the *Cunard Line* known by its distinctive single red funnel topped with black, and their ships the *S.S. Carmania, Carinthia* and *Franconia* – all ending in "ia". The White Star Line was marked by yellow funnels topped with black, all its fleet had names ending in "ic" – the *Celtic, Baltic* and *Majestic*. The two funnelled *Celtic* ended her days in tragic fashion as she was wrecked on the Cow Rock, just off Roches Point. It was a foul night and she had a full complement of passengers and cargo. Fortunately, the weather improved and the passengers were taken off, as was most of the cargo.

Later, these two shipping lines were joined by the US line, with ships called the *Washington* and the *Lincoln*. These had black funnels with red, white and blue bands on top. Each line employed their own pilot who lived in Queenstown and also had accommodation at Roches Point. The *Cunard* and *White Star* pilots occupied the now ruined houses on the high ground behind the terrace. The US line pilots took over the square tower, which still stand next to the coastguard signalling tower.

These pilots made the journey from Queenstown by open long boats propelled by four strong oarsmen. Waiting until their ships were sighted they then put to sea and boarded the liner off the Point through a door set well down on the side of the ship. The pilot would then guide the huge ship (20,000 tonnes approx.) usually to the anchorage beyond the forts and near where the oil refinery pier is today. Sometimes, in good weather, they were brought to an area just off the Point. There the Liners would be met by a passenger tender from Queenstown that would transfer passengers, baggage and mail ashore.

This would take a few hours and the pilot would then guide the ship out of the harbour and some way out to sea. There, he would be picked up by the long boat and rowed back to Queenstown. In bad weather or fog it was a hazardous undertaking and, on more than one occasion, the pilot got a free ride to New York and back! While these proud ships were wonderful to look at as they moved majestically along by day, at night they were quite something else, a fantastic fairyland of lights on the dark waters.

We children were great ship watchers and we would always be on the look-out for the pilot's long boat to find out when and what ships were due and then who sighted her first, and of course which ship it was.

Other regular visitors were the Kelly coal boats, distinctive in design with their narrow beam, two masts and black funnel at stern with a red and white band. Suttons of Cork were part of the Kelly empire then and they had their own coal fleet.

Apart from the Coastguards' and their families' comings and goings, there were other inhabitants at the Point. Next to our summer home lived quite a marvel – an old lady over 100 years old, and her daughter who took care of her. On sunny days she would sit at her front door enjoying the sun and quietly smoking her clay pipe. This, to us, was quite amazing – a lady who smoked a pipe! In those days few women smoked at all! When, at the ripe old age of 105, the good Lord called her home, her daughter – who was nearly an octogenarian at that stage, sold up and departed for the USA to marry her lifetime sweetheart. He, much as he loved her, refused to share his life with her and her mother.

Then there was the Roche family. My friend Michael was the 'pet' of the household having been more or less 'adopted' by his Aunts for companionship sake. His father was a lighthouse keeper. He and I were around the same age and became more or less inseparable when I was on Summer holidays at the Point. He was not alone a fine looking, well built lad, but also of a grand nature and disposition. Michael's grandfather, a kindly man with a full white beard, enjoyed to sit in his garden of roses and take the sun. He and my father, who also had a grey beard, were great companions. There also was Michael's Uncle Bill, a bachelor with a charming manner, uncanny skills, and a great ladies' man. He was in great demand as a fortune-teller, and could read your future in your tea leaves – often with uncanny accuracy. He could do likewise telling your fortune with the cards. He was an excellent mechanic and could mend practically anything and when it came to fishing, he was far and away the best around.

Presiding over the household were Michael's two aunts – Amy and Bunty. They also had the job of tending to the weather station.

Twice a day they visited the white, fenced-off rectangle in the green which surrounded the box-like structure in the centre containing the instruments for measuring the rainfall, temperature, the rise and fall of the barometer, a small weather vane that recorded the velocity of the wind. This information was then sent to the weather station in Dublin and was the forerunner of the Meteorological weather centre now situated on top of the hill as you approach the Point, but no longer used today.

There was another aunt of Michael's called Emily who had a superior position in Thompsons, the bakers and restaurateurs in Cork, and she came to the Point most weekends. All the Roche family had an air of quality about them. They spoke well, were highly intelligent and were great neighbours and friends. The Point also had a Post Office run by the FitzMahony family, next to them was Jim Hynes and his wife Mary Ann, and next to them lived the Coleman brothers Mike and Jack, nephews of Mary Ann.

Looking north from Roches Point, the outer harbour was a mile wide to Crosshaven on the western side and narrowed to half that distance where it was dominated by Carlisle Fort at the Point side and Camden Fort on the other. These forts were manned by British military forces. Beautiful White Bay lay at the feet of Carlisle, golden sand, caves and a wonderful view of the Point and the lighthouse one mile south. The inner harbour held Spike Island, housing another military garrison and Haulbowline where there was a naval base. Behind the two rose Queenstown, dominated by its beautiful Cathedral.

One of the Colemans, Jack, who walked with a limp, had a job with Irish Lights, which these days sounds very strange. There were two paraffin fuelled navigation lights situated above White Bay on the perimeter of Carlisle Fort. Jack's job was to keep these lights working. Regardless of the weather, he trudged a mile and a half to White Bay every evening to light the warning lights and at dawn returned to extinguish them. Technological advances have since made those lights unnecessary.

CHAPTER 3

OTHER ATTRACTIONS

A nother big attraction at the Point was the lighthouse itself, manned by a Head Keeper and two other keepers (later increased to three). It was quite a thrill to be invited to the lantern and to watch the lights being lit. These consisted of burners fuelled by paraffin converted into gas by heat and this gas burned in the mantels. Getting it started involved a blow lamp to obtain the necessary heat, and once the mantels were going, having wound the mechanism, the huge bee-hive shaped lantern of polished glass lenses would come alive. The rotating screen meant that the light disappeared from view for some time and this formed the beam that is visible from as far away as the Old Head of Kinsale.

The other great attraction was the fog horn – worked by compressed air generated by one of two big compressors, each with an enormous fly wheel and these were also fuelled by paraffin. The blast of the horn was quite shattering if you stood beneath it and the echo resounded along the rocky shore.

On one memorable occasion, both the generators refused to function, it was night-time and the whole population of able-bodied men was enlisted to turn the huge fly wheels manually. Whilst this timing of the blast was much slower, it produced some kind of warning for the ships. The men's hard labour lasted about four hours until the mechanical skill of the keepers got one of the engines functioning again. There was also another beacon functioning five miles out at sea provided by the Daunt Rock lightship, and this flashed a red warning light. This was serviced from Queenstown by a friend of my fathers, Ruby Robinson, and on one memorable occasion it was arranged that we would visit. Ruby anchored off the Point and sent the punt to fetch us and off we set.

It was not a rough day but there was always the Atlantic swell and when we pulled alongside the lightship it was evident that it would not be easy to board the vessel. Ruby and my father had to clamber up a rope ladder and one of the seamen hoisted me aloft and another on the lightship hauled me aboard.

It was quite different than any ship I have ever been on, with an extraordinarily wide beam, no funnel and this enormous structure mid-ship on which was mounted the warning lantern. Whatever way it was anchored I do not know, but beside it lifting up and down on the swell it also moved about clockwise and anti-clockwise and if you did not get sea-sick, then you were a true sailor. Both my father and I passed the test. To occupy time on the lightship was not easy, so the crew met this challenge by knitting. They were expert knitters and made beautiful pullovers. They also made model ships, miraculously getting them into bottles. This was done by making all rigging so that it can be folded around the hull and then pushed into the bottle. Then all the rigging is raised upright again by pulling on one slender thread. It takes hours of painstaking skill to achieve this. All the crew were avid readers also and could converse widely on a wide variety of subjects. We enjoyed our visit which lasted several hours. Then, with the stores replenished and the old crew taken aboard, we departed for home. It was a visit I can never forget.

Of course there is no Daunt Rock lightship today, it has long since been replaced by a buoy. The lighthouse-keepers had another attraction for us involving buoys. The *S.S. Teragh* would come to unloaded buoys used for marking shipping lanes and these had been lifted from the sea and were encrusted with thousands of mussels. They were towed ashore and hauled by a crane onto what was known as the "Buoy Yard". The lighthouse-keeper's job, for which they got extra pay, was to scale these and repaint them. This took a long long time and then the *Teragh* would come and lift them off again. The station was often inspected by head inspectors who also arrived on the *S.S. Teragh*, which resembled a private yacht with her fiddle bow and raking lines. It would anchor off the Point and the inspectors then rowed ashore and everything in the lighthouse had to be spick, span and shining on that day. We always found it a great fascination watching all the comings and goings.

The Inner Harbour Sentinels

The canteen at Carlisle Fort was franchised to a Mr "Spud" Murphy, a family friend, and we often walked the couple of miles to visit, he also arranged an odd visit to the canteen, where the British Forces, nicknamed "Tommies", made us welcome – though at times we found it hard to understand their brand of their own language!

Now our friend had a very vicious Kerry Blue dog and one eventful night the dog broke loose. Not liking men in uniform, it chased a group returning to barracks. This would not have been too bad had not two of them been Officers, who in desperation, climbed up a tree where the dog held them until morning. So, poor Spud Murphy lost his franchise!

Even today I still think of their soldiers' favourite "tummy-filler", a bar of Fry's Chocolate Cream sandwiched between two slices of bread and butter – not as awful as it seems either should you be tempted to try it out, and certainly very filling!

The "tommies" ran regular dances and local girls were very welcome. Many a romance flourished, including that of my own sister. She found herself in love and in due course saw the world as a soldier's wife visiting Gibraltar, Malta and the Far East, ending up in Hong Kong where tragic events overtook her and her family.

Her husband was in charge of the heavy artillery defences in Hong Kong and she and their two boys were evacuated to Manilla, New Zealand and then to Australia. He fell to the Japanese and was a prisoner of war and put aboard the *Lisbon Maru* – a Japanese prison ship for slave labour in Japan. This ship was torpedoed by a US submarine and sank not far off shore. Many of the prisoners managed to escape alive to China and some found their way home after the war only to find that they had been posted missing and that their wives had re-married. My sister's husband, unfortunately, went with the ship.

Communications between the Forts, Spike Island and the mainland were maintained by a small steamer, the *S.S. Wyndham*. If you could get a pass on this, it was one of the easy ways of getting to Roches Point – a train to Queenstown, the steamer to Carlisle, and walk two miles. Of course, there was a paddle steamer on some days running from Albert Quay to Aghada pier, then a taxi or a horse-trip to get to the Point. There was also a train to Crosshaven which was a lovely scenic journey, then a walk to Grabal Bay and a friend with a boat would row you across. We had to use all methods!

For us children, the Forts had only one interest – target practice. There were a few rather large guns in both forts and the *Wyndham* would tow a floating target consisting of a white super structure mounted on a small boat, using needless to say, a very long rope! She would go out to sea for about three or four miles and then the guns would open up. That was a day to have a friendly lighthouse-keeper who would lend you his excellent telescope or spy-glass. These were so powerful you could read the time on Cobh Cathedral, five miles away.

By the telescope on the lighthouse wall you would have a perfect grandstand seat of what seemed like a real war, and great fun! Sometimes they had a night shoot and this was very spectacular. One unforgettable night, when the *Wyndham* was proceeding homeward, still towing the intact illuminated target, her Captain and crew of three got more than they ever expected – so did the people of Roches Point and those living around Fountainstown and Church Bay. What happened was that a British battleship with a Rear-Admiral on board was due at Haulbowline and had dropped anchor for the night just off Templebreedy Fort – just above Church Bay. The old sea dog, seeing what was going on, thought it was an excellent time to test the efficiency of the ship's guns. He ordered the Captain to sound a full alert, man the guns, and leave off a full broadside at the target. That's just what they did and blew the target to smithereens! They scared the living daylights out of the *Wyndham* captain and crew and broke every window in the Point, including cracking some of the outside panes in the lighthouse.

We did not know what had hit us and thought war had been declared. People were running all over the place in a half-dressed state screaming and shouting. It took us all a few days to recover. The *Admiralty* had to foot the bill – and not an inconsiderable one either.

Fishing, Yachting and Sailing ships

The weekends were the fullest. There were the yachts from the Royal Yacht Club in Crosshaven, these were beautiful to watch, particularly in the shorter races confined to the harbour, and it was usually then that the liners arrived. Again, a telescope from the lighthouse-keeper was most desirable. On one memorable occasion, when rounding the harbour buoy, a helmsman took it too close just as a squall struck and the main sail of the yacht got entangled on the buoy. One of the crew jumped onto the buoy, and as he did, the boat broke free and he was left clinging on for dear life. He was stuck for over an hour and a half before being rescued by a motor launch from Crosshaven. Rough days provided the best spectacle and I saw at least two yachts and a motor launch being driven onto the rocks at Carlisle, all of which became total wrecks, as far as I know, but with no loss of life.

For us there was never a dull moment and we did lots of other things besides liner and yacht watching. There are some marvellous pools, both on the Atlantic and harbour side, ideal for sailing model boats and we spent many a happy hour at this, imagining that we were captaining real sailing ships. Three pools, still there today, were our favourites. Two were Atlantic pools and lay almost in line with the pilot's house. The other one was very deep and lay in line with the end Coastguard house on the foreshore. Then there was the shrimping and periwinkle gathering and always a chance of finding something of interest washed in by the tide. It was in this way that I first discovered grapefruit, but we did not know what exactly it was as they were certainly not on sale in the shops in those days. Very often you would find a crate half-full of oranges or apples, the crates were useful for the fire. We found such odd things as false teeth and spectacles frequently – God help the owners! I suppose the articles fell overboard. Of course, we loved the water, though, strange to say, we were not great swimmers.

However, far and away the best fun was crabbing and fishing. Watching and knowing the tide was most important, especially the ebb tide, when the sea has receded furthest from the shore. We were armed with a gaff which was made by getting a stair-rod, heating the end in the fire and fashioning a tight inverted "U" shape at one end and an "L" shape at the other. One point on the "U" was sharpened carefully and the "L" end was fitted into a hole bored in a long brush handle. This latter fitting was then carefully bound with wire and that was a gaff! The sport was to push the gaff into holes in the rocks and root out the crabs or lobsters that frequented them. The further out you could get, the better chance of getting a big lobster or a big crab. Hence, the importance of knowing the ebb tides. We caught plenty but the bulk of our catch were crabs. A crab will hang on to the rocks until very often it loses a pincer or an arm, but a lobster will decide to make a bolt for it, and this is what we had to watch out for. It emerges at lightning speed, travelling backwards, pushing water backwards out of its many openings on its scaly sides – almost jet propulsion – and you have to be ready to grab it then.

The trick is to catch it by the back before it catches you, remembering it can break a finger as easy as you would break a match. Once I recall that we caught a huge lobster and took him triumphantly home to my sister. She, the poor girl, had never cooked a lobster before but somebody told her to put it in cold water and cook it. So we put it into a pot and departed but, when the pot got too hot the lobster lifted the lid, crawled out and fell to the floor. Despite my sister's fear she managed to get it back in again using a pair of tongs and she cooked it beautifully – with about fourteen pounds of scrap iron on top of the lid! We knew our crabs very well and the female crab was the better prize even though she was smaller. She was recognisable by the wide maw – that is a heart shaped mark on her lower side. The reason that she was preferred was that you could cook not alone her claws but all of the inside. Baking it covered in breadcrumbs was lovely. The jack crab, distinctive for its narrow pointed heart shaped maw mark on its underside, was only useful for its huge claws and you had to have a good pincers to get the flesh out of them.

Very often we would get a soft crab, that is a developing crab which, having got rid of its shell, only had a soft shell in the meantime. These were very good bait for catching fish. If you were a real fisherman the big attraction would be to get soft crabs and fish for bass off the flat rocks. These flat rocks were quite easy to distinguish and lie just beyond the stony beach at the eastward side of the Atlantic shore. Bass were usually caught on the incoming tide, so here again you had to watch the tide very carefully. Most of the other fishing was done by means of artificial bait (red, amber or black eels for catching pollock and spinners for catching mackerel), and was usually done underneath the lighthouse. Now I mentioned earlier that Bill Roche, Michael's Uncle, was the best fisherman around. While we would all be gathered under the lighthouse, Bill would stand like a billy-goat on a ledge, sniffing the air (we always said he could smell the fish). Then, after a little while Bill would appear at a different place, perhaps over by the Cow and Calf rock off Roches Point.

The real difference was that in no time Bill would be catching pollock while we would be catching nothing except the seaweed at the bottom of the gully. When the mackerel arrived, people would descend from all around and would catch so many mackerel that they could not carry them home. These mackerel would be dumped at the side of the road and the place would stink of rotting fish for the mackerel season. Now pollock and mackerel were one thing, but conger eels were something very different. This was real he-man stuff and generally the sport of the lighthouse-keepers. The best place was right underneath the lighthouse, where there was a deep gully and a cave, and here these formidable monsters frequented. The preparation to catch one of them was a detailed professional job. A very large strong steel hook on an equally strong but slender chain and a heavy duty line and float was needed. A mackerel was secured firmly onto the hook and the right location selected. This is where expertise counted, knowing where they were was always a great mystery to us. Then the baited hook was carefully lowered into the water and the game began.

This could be long or short, but when the eel did strike, the strain was enormous and it could take half an hour or more to finally haul the monster up on the rocks with the aid of a gaff and what a prize it was! Six feet or more of struggling fury that had to be killed quickly before it bit your foot off. It had a reddish mane of spiky fins running from the head down its back, and the mouth with its protruding bottom jaw had a terrible array of teeth. Some of the keepers enjoyed the flesh, which is white, but the real enjoyment was catching the brutes. We watched in awe and only came close to inspect when we were sure that the creature was really dead.

Once, while Michael and I were near the buoy-yard we spotted an unusual object in a pool. I poked it with a stick and it flashed across the pool with amazing speed and the pool turned black. The blackness cleared after some time but it took even longer to locate the object, as it seemed to assume the reddish colour of the pool! We were fascinated and ran for help to catch this unusual fish which we eventually got into a large bucket and then transferred to a bath full of sea water.

My father said it was a small octopus and a most unusual find in such cold waters. This was confirmed when a call to University

College Cork brought an expert who took it away. The octopus was darkish brown, almost black in colour, about one foot in diameter and had eight tentacles. There was an article in the newspaper about it and my name was mentioned; I felt very proud and at least two feet taller!

Chapter 4

UNUSUAL EVENTS

One day Michael, while returning from school in Whitegate, stopped to watch a Free State soldier who was on sentry duty at the old Coastguard Station – the Coastguards were long gone. He was busily engaged in cleaning his rifle, the magazine was detached and lying on the ground with some empty shell cases. There was some conversation and Michael said that he was going to take a few of the empty shells whereupon the soldier, more in fun than otherwise, said, "If you do I'll shoot you," at the same time pointing his rifle at Michael who continued to pick up a few shells.

What the soldier was not aware of was that although the magazine was removed from the gun there *was* a bullet in the breach. When he pulled the trigger Michael got the bullet at close range in his right arm.

The end result was amputation of the right arm and, alas, a fine boy was now left with only his left arm. If Michael was not a determined and very strong lad he could have been like a handicapped person all his life but he was made of much sturdier stuff and resolved to carry on life as usual. He soon learnt to write with his left hand, to fish and go crabbing, to play tennis, and later on in life to shoot and to drive. He developed immense strength in his left arm and could not be beaten at wrestling, which was a popular past-time, even by lads twice his age.

Eventually, when his grandfather, Uncle Bill and aunts had all died, Michael still stayed on where he was employed in the newly developed meteorological station.

Trabolgan Estate owned all the surrounding land. It was the home of Lord Fermoy and he maintained the full status of landowner, employing house staff and game-keepers. One of these, surnamed

Gavin, lived in the small house, still standing in good condition, next to the car park above White Bay. There was a gate across the road there and you had to get his permission to proceed further as you now entered private land. Later on, Trabolgan came on the market and was purchased by Captain Clarke of the Clarke tobacco family in Cork. Who has not heard of Clarke's Perfect Plug? And many's the two ounce block I cut and rubbed for my father's pipe. Captain Clarke was the first I had heard of who succeeded in breeding pheasants successfully in captivity. Michael and I often walked across the field to view the beautiful old house. As we walked across, we often disturbed a pheasant. They would wait until you were almost about to step on them and then take off at such a rate and with such flapping of wings that they would scare the living daylights out of you. Overlooking Foyle Bay was an old circular watch-tower and this Captain Clarke converted into a smoking lodge.

The Foyle, nestling under the next mini-headland on the Atlantic side of the Point, was much easier to get to than it is now. In fact, a road had been cut to allow horses and carts to get to the bay. This was to facilitate the gathering of seaweed much then used as a fertiliser. For some reason the Foyle seemed to attract seaweed and after rough weather it came ashore in huge quantities and lay six to eight feet deep. There were, and still are, some fine caves in the Foyle and these were frequented by otters. Mr FitzMahony and Bill Roche made many an excursion to shoot an otter and often brought home a prize. The pelt could be sold to a Cork furrier who would convert it into a nice stole, much appreciated by the ladies then.

Near the end of the old road to the Foyle, there was a huge crater, still visible today. One memorable day during World War I, the wall and adjoining rocks were blown sky high by a big mine which was washed in and which detonated on the rocks. Fortunately, it occurred when the area was deserted.

White Bay, surely the finest sandy bay in the harbour, was another favourite haunt. At one time, long, long ago, there was a small fishing community living there but only one house was occupied in our time by the McTigue family. Its ruins are still there now. Nearby was a corrugated iron bungalow then occupied by a retired seaman and his wife. They were a lovely couple and one would never be allowed to leave without a scone and a glass of goat's milk. They were the Colemans and we always called that part of the bay Coleman's Bay.

My brother Bill, at this time, was working and had purchased a motor boat. He and four or five of his pals from Cork Boat Club would visit for weekends. On one such trip we all walked across to White Bay for a swim as there was a path across the cliffs. When we reached our destination I did not immediately tog off while the other lads did, but as I wandered across the bay I saw a bottle sticking out of the edge of the water.

I had a sudden impulse to have a shot at it with a stone. I wasn't a bad shot, but no great expert, so much to my surprise and delight I struck it and broke the bottle in two with my first shot! My joy was quickly turned to horror and anguish as one of the lads emerged from the rocks shouting "I'll be first in". He ran full speed for the water and stepped onto the broken bottle. He let out a sudden cry of pain as he fell to the ground with his big toe nearly severed. Plenty of blood stained the sand. Fortunately, we had a student doctor from UCC with us and he knew what to do. We had to almost carry him the mile back to Roches Point where he got proper medical attention. Due to the initial care of our student, he fully recovered. He never said a word of blame or condemnation to me and I thought it was very fine of him, indeed we were very good friends until his death. I never took pot shots at bottles or anything else again!

A Guardian Angel with a Black Belt

Bill and some of his friends also used to go camping in Crosshaven, a popular seaside resort for all Corkonians. There were usually eight big lads and this number could nearly double at the weekends.

They had a large bell tent and a small oblong tent, which they called a "Bivy". The latter was pitched on a slight slope and accommodated six for sleeping.On one occasion I was invited along for a long weekend.

On this excursion, the chap at the end of the slope began to feel the pressure of the other five bodies impelling him towards one of the lower tent poles. He soon grew tired of this and arose to find a space to sleep in at the top end of the tent. The next lad in line soon did the same and they ended up taking turns moving all night. It could be called rotational sleeping – not to be recommended! But we were young lads out to enjoy ourselves and it was part of the excitement of camping. We swam, played football, and indulged in lots of horseplay. Being younger I was involved in this and the bigger lads had a contest to see who could muscle me. To "muscle" meant to put your two hands under the "victims" arms and to try to lift him up until your arms were rigid.

Everyone took turns trying, but then on one attempt, while being lowered to the ground, my braces caught in a belt buckle and both my trouser buttons popped off! Another lad helped me out by sewing the buttons back on, without removing my trousers. This seemed fine until I tried to undress for bed that night. The buttons were sewn to both my trousers and my shirt! As the saying goes "I was all sewn up."

I enjoyed camping with Bill but then I began to suffer a big setback in my otherwise very satisfactory life. 1922 turned out to be a bad year, because at the end of one such weekend I developed a severe pain in my head. This got so bad that I was rushed to hospital in Cork. The doctor ordered me to stay in. I thought I had sunstroke but it was much worse. I had meningitis, almost an incurable complaint then. I was in the South Fever Hospital on Douglas Road, commonly known as "The Workhouse" as that was what the buildings were originally used for. I knew I was very ill and I prayed very hard. I had always been brought up to worship God in the Protestant faith and my father and I were regular church-goers at St

Paul's Church. Here, all the family were members of the Choir and I also sang anthems. The Church building later became part of Musgrave Bros.

I also knew many others were praying too. Our prayers were answered by the most unangelic looking Guardian Angel imaginable – namely the matron. She was a nun of masculine proportions and wore a black habit with a wide leather belt, and was feared by all. The doctors were in despair as very little was known about meningitis. The matron, however, felt she could do something – and she did. She ordered some sort of a lotion to be applied to my back that caused huge blisters. I suffered almost intolerable pain and my back resembled a piece of meat hanging in a butcher's shop, but it worked. The process seemed to draw the poison out of my system and miraculously I began to recover. I was in hospital for six long weeks during which one patient in the ward died which, needless to say, frightened me. Nurses were very good and pulled my bed to the window to let me see the green fields. On recovery I had five or six different doctors calling to see the "miracle" as very few people in those days survived meningitis. One extraordinary effect which it had was on my eyes. I could see double and would try to grab what really wasn't there! I got plenty of jiving about this, being told to water down the drinks, etc.

I was packed off to Roches Point to recuperate and I missed twelve valuable months at school. But I was glad to be alive and fully recovered. I was full of thankfulness to my Maker for this and felt I must have had my health restored with some definite purpose in mind. I decided then that I would live my life to the full – I have and I am still full of thankfulness.

I was very fond of sport and played football (soccer) with The Church Lads Brigade, of which I was a very keen member. I also enjoyed cricket and upset the field as I was a left-handed batsman. They were very happy days as I was one of the few who liked study, found school interesting and was always a good worker. I became very interested in music and when the St Nicholas Brass

Band was revived, I became a very enthusiastic member and played the euphonium (tenor tuba). We practised weekly, played in the various churches on special occasions and gave recitals at annual Boys Brigade demonstrations.

There were three McCarthy brothers in the band, two being twins. All were talented musicians. One of the twins played the euphonium next to me and his brother played the horn. When they tired of one they would change over and were such good musicians you would never notice. Indeed I never knew which twin I had next to me. They enjoyed the confusion immensely.

CHAPTER 5

THE "TROUBLES"

P oliticaly, Ireland was at a crossroads at this time. The First World War was over and the nationalistic spirit was waxing ever stronger. In the general elections of December 1918, Sinn Féin carried 78 seats but refused to take their seats in Westminster as they would not take the Oath of Allegiance. In January 1919 a meeting was held in Dublin, constituting themselves Dáil Éireann. A declaration of independence was issued and the Republic was established. Civil war flared as the British government strove to repress the movement. I knew little of politics at the time but I was acutely aware of the increasing military activity in Cork city. Open backed small motor trucks known as Crossley Tenders full of police whizzed about and we were aware of the presence in the streets of the "Black & Tans" and "Auxiliaries" (mercenaries hired by the British Government). Black and Tans wore black uniforms and tan accessories and Auxiliaries wore khaki.

They were ruthless men and trained gunmen and I saw evidence of this one day while coming from school. I was crossing Parnell Bridge near the City Hall and there were two "Black & Tans" carrying two guns each. One gun was slung low on the right leg for a quick draw. They were stopping and searching every male adult who crossed the bridge and they took pleasure in frightening people and demonstrating their prowess. One of them demanded a sixpence piece from a man that he had stopped. A six-pence was only twenty centimetres in diameter but he tossed it in the air with his left hand, drew his gun in a flash and blew the coin out of the air. A dead shot! Then one Sunday while I was coming from church there was a scuffle outside a pub, a gun was drawn, a shot fired and a man fell – shot in the head. Miraculously, he was not killed as the bullet only grazed his forehead.

Bill had a near brush with death around this time. The British forces had taken over the County Club building on the South Channel at the junction of Grand Parade and South Mall. The inexperienced Officer in Command paraded his men in front of the building every morning and this did not go unnoticed by the IRA.

They mounted a machine-gun on the back of an open truck and made a dash along Sullivan's Quay on the opposite bank. The machine-gun opened fire and shot the soldiers, then a machine-gun on the roof of the building returned fire. During this my brother had been walking along the quay. He saw the truck roaring past and an unfortunate horse fell by him with a gaping wound in its side. He was then pushed violently to the ground and a voice beside him shouted "Lie flat!", as the bullets ripped a swathe in the wall above their heads! The man who saved his life was the driver of the horse and dray and happened to be an ex-army man who had plenty of experience in similar situations in World War One.

Never to be forgotten was the burning of Cork and I can still see Patrick's Street that fateful Sunday morning, 11 December 1920. Practically all one side of the street was in ruins but one tall wall remained upright with an iron safe protruding from it. During the following days, attempts were made to topple the wall and I saw one such episode.

A very strong rope had been secured to the wall by the use of a fire escape ladder and this rope was then tied to a tractor. When put into motion, it slowly began to move forward as the rope tightened, the wall leaned but did not fall. It actually brought the tractor to a halt and slowly began to drag it backwards! It was quite incredible. In the end, explosion experts had to be called in to topple it. Many said that this fire was the best thing that ever happened to Patrick's Street. Fine new buildings rose out of the ashes. To this day one side of "Pana" (Patrick's Street as called by all true Corkonians) remains quite old-fashioned. The habit of nick-naming was common and most streets had their own nicknames. Patrick's Street was called "Pana", Barrack's Street was "Barraka", and King Street (now McCurtain Street) was "Kinga".

Girls – Girls – Girls

Around this time I began to realise that girls were different from boys. They had longer hair, softer skin, more subtle colouring and were a different shape. They also possessed sharper voices, had a magnetic effect and were very interesting!

One of my friends had a tennis court which I often visited. We had to earn our game by spending an hour fruit-picking from the large orchard and then it was tennis or croquet. One of his sisters, Lucy, and I were very good friends. The family was large, some 10 in all, and when invited to stay for tea it was quite an experience. We sat, boys on one side and girls on the other, at a full billiard table covered over. The father sat at one end and the mother at the other. You only spoke when spoken to and were often glad when the meal ended. But the food was excellent, and the game and the companionship of lovely Lucy was well worth it all.

Another one of my friends, MacDonald, had twin sisters Jean and Alice. They were full of high spirits and we were all mad about both. The trouble was if you dated one, you could never be quite sure which one of the twins would turn up. If you thought you were with Alice and, having confessed ardent love all evening and just kissed her goodnight, she'd say, "Well, I'll tell Alice all about it"! The trouble was you never did know. They certainly made fools out of us and enjoyed it.

And so my school days slipped away and now I was attending a business school. This was a well known establishment known as Cobanus Business Academy situated at South Terrace, Cork, specialising in teaching business practices, book keeping and typing. I attended for two years and did well in all subjects, whilst there was no precise certification in those days, the fact that you were a successful pupil of the Academy was a valuable assett. The girls were much more attractive than the work and two lads, in particular, made the most of it. The father of one was a well-known solicitor who worked in the city. Consequently, his car lay idly parked on the South Mall – that is until his son decided that it was such a waste of a car not to use it all day. He and his pal began inviting the girls to go for a spin, cutting school for the day, of course. This went on for some time until one day, being more interested in the close presence of his companion, the driver lost his concentration and hit the ditch. There was hell to pay, no car awaiting as his father emerged from the office. The father had heard some reports and putting two and two together phoned the school and learned the worst. We were all very glad that we hadn't participated.

Book 2
Musgrave Brothers

CHAPTER 6

AN UNUSUAL ENTRY

This was 1926 and on Christmas Eve I called into Musgrave Brothers, now in their splendid new premises in Cornmarket Street, to see if my father and I could go home together. The office was open-plan and consisted of six long sloping-top desks at which the staff sat on high stools, and this was fronted by a long mahogany counter.

I met my father outside the counter and while he explained that he would be an hour or so longer, John L. Musgrave came through the swinging doors behind us and said, "How long will you be, Charlie ?" On being told the situation he at once turned to me and said, "Come with me and we will find something to keep you occupied." We went to his office whereupon he called his secretary, Miss Edie Dearnley, and said "Edie, this is young Creighton. He is waiting for his father and you can set him the usual test papers." Having made me comfortable at a desk in her office that backed onto his, she produced a neat file and set out what was to be done. I was not aware that what I was being asked to do to pass the hour was the usual method devised by John L. Musgrave to ascertain the ability of intending applicants for a job with the company. Consequently, I was completely relaxed. Had I know the truth, I might not have been! I had to copy several paragraphs to test my handwriting, write a row of figures from one to ten, and price and tot several long invoices. Biscuit invoices were quite tricky as each tin was a different weight, i.e. a five and three-quarter pound tin at nine pence three farthings a pound, etc.

There were discounts to be calculated and deducted off each invoice and on some there was carriage – so much per hundred-weight – added on. There were long and short tots. It was a long

time before calculators were invented and accurate mental arithmetic was vital. I had almost finished the test when my father
arrived and we both went home and had a very happy Christmas.
No more was said about the Christmas Eve event until mid-
February, when one evening my father informed me that I had
done well and that a job in Musgrave Brothers would be available
soon.

So it was on that morning of 7 March 1927, I reported for work
and was assigned to Miss Madge Donovan in the grocery section. I
was rigged out in light brown overalls, as were all males. The girls
were similarly clad in dark blue. It was a very fine and impressive
warehouse stretching to Brown's Street, where the stables were situated. It was all one level and there was an area in the centre
where goods could be loaded and unloaded under the same roof.
Two thirds was for storage and one third for compiling orders.

The orders were assembled on rows of counters about three feet
high and the goods were stocked on the shelves beneath. Visual
control was effected over the area by various edifices, like the
bridge on a ship, situated at good vantage points. The area from
which business was drawn covered all Munster and parts of
Connaught – west of Galway, and parts of Kilkenny. There was one
agent who covered Kilkenny and then six full-time representatives.
These men were very important as personalities counted and the
commercial traveller was a very respected member of the business
community. He was the real connection between the customer and
the business. Many only did business with the representative and
had no real contact with anyone else. Because of this, no representative was allowed an exclusive area (such as all one county), the
reason being that once he had a grip of the trade he might transfer
to another distributor to his own advantage and to the detriment of
the previous distributor. John L. Musgrave, however, made it his
business to personally know all the larger retailers and this was a
necessary safeguard.

Motor cars were by now becoming an essential part of business life and all commercial travellers had one of these much-envied possessions. The ordinary citizen, however, had to rely on public transport, the horse and trap or cart, and the reliable bicycle. All shops were counter shops and the traveller was advised in advance by post of the approximate time he should call. He was responsible for obtaining orders and collecting cash, which was lodged daily in the nearest bank. Orders were posted each night. As a consequence, the flow of orders could be quite erratic, a glut arriving one day and none at all the next. The system revolved around each representative's journey comprising of a four-week-cycle. This was known as a "book". When I started work, orders were handwritten and *not* in duplicate form. These sheets of orders were pasted into a book and copied by hand onto pads that the order-compiler made by cutting up sheets of blank paper and nailing them to a piece of timber. This could lead to an item being wrongly transcribed or not transcribed at all. Labels were written by office staff for unbroken items, i.e. case lots. Broken items had to be assembled by staff on the counters.

Manufacturers were yet to co-operate by packing in saleable amounts and tended to opt for as big a pack as possible. Matches were in large cases containing 36 gross and they frequently went on fire if a case was roughly handled. Each order had to be divided by a piece of plywood on stands and the label written out and clipped on. Two reliable people then toured the area, one calling from the original order and the other checking. Items that were temporarily out of stock were itemised on the back of the label. Once checked, each order was loaded onto a four-wheel trolley and transferred to the packing bay. This consisted of a long row of bays into which the order was placed to await packing into tea chests. Straw was used to protect fragile items and glass. The order was then married up with any full case lots in the despatch area and each day these were despatched by rail to all destinations. In the meantime, the checkers handwrote each order into a Day Book, these were then extended and totted by my father and the invoice typed in due course. A very labour intensive and slow process, but with great emphasis on having no errors. Miss Madge Donovan was in charge of Book No.7, the traveller was Mr Jerome McAuliffe, who also had an agency for Clarke's, the tobacco manufacturers.

The Nuts and Bolts of the Business

Trainees were called "slags" and as I quickly found out, they were worked hard by their charge-hands. When not assembling orders, there were always goods to be weighed out in seven, fourteen, or twenty-eight pound paper bags. Washing soda, bread soda, several varieties of rice, tapioca, sago, currants, sultanas, seedless raisins, caraway seed, all-spice, and pepper were just some of the items that were bagged. The pepper was kept in the back store and one had to be careful while stooping into the bins, because if another "slag" was nearby he might push you in. What a state you would be in then with the pepper up your nose, down your throat and in your eyes.

Sweet confectionery was stocked in the Fancy Room on the next floor but assembled by the grocery staff. This meant going up in the lift and the chance to getting a few sweets from a broken box. Someone must have broken the boxes and if they happened to be discovered they would be instantly dismissed. Yet, I never knew this to happen. All other goods stocked in the Fancy Room such as hardware, etc., were assembled by the staff there and added to the grocery order in due course. This meant that the orders had to be copied by the Fancy Room staff first, further delaying the process for the Grocery staff. Unless the compilation worked in unison, orders could be delayed and this often led to friction.

The "Broken" Grocery section was controlled by Mr Tom MacBrateney (Mr Mac as we called him), who also was the overall grocery buyer. He was a tall well-built man and ruled with great authority commanding the respect of all. Control was enforced with probably the most sarcastic tongue I was ever to experience. Each charge-hand was responsible for maintaining stock under four counters. If this was found wanting, he or she was in trouble. On one such occasion, when asked by Mr Mac why this occurred the misfortunate young man in question answered, "I thought there was enough for the day, Sir". "You are not paid to think, I am paid to think and you are paid to do the work" was the withering reply. Sometime later the same chap, Carl Humphries, reported to Mr Mac that they were completely out of stock of a particular item and was answered with "You should have notified me days ago, why don't you use your brain?" Humphries by now had had enough. "You told me that you were paid to do the thinking and all I was paid to do was work," was the reply. There was no response to this but the retort was not forgotten because any dirty job or overtime to be worked was given to the unfortunate Humphries.

The last male recruited always got the job of collecting the post at the Post Office's sorting department in Pembroke Street at 8.15am and had to deliver it strictly at 8.30am to John L. Musgrave, and then assist him to sort it by department. This was a job which I duly got. The sloping desk and high stool were standard in all offices and letters were kept from sliding off by using glass paper-weights.

Mr Musgrave was a strict disciplinarian, both with himself and others. He lived at Hayfield House, College Road and he was an early riser. He walked to work regardless of the weather, which took about twenty-five minutes. Having sorted the post, he attended to his personal mail and at 9.30am started off on his departmental business. First to the Fancy Room across the landing from the Offices, then down the main stairs to Mr MacBrateney and on to Mr Tim McCarthy, the warehouse manager. Finally, he went up the stairs at the end of the warehouse to Mr Alan Wilkie, tea-buyer and manager of the tea department. With each he briefly discussed any problems or queries and having had a cup of tea in the dining-room near the tea depart-ment, he retraced his steps and picked up the answers as he went.

He moved so fast you almost had to be a mind-reader to

decipher what he was referring to and everyone had to be on their toes. All staff had a mid-day meal – main course of meat and vegetables, a pudding of rice, tapioca or similar and a cup of tea – for which nine shillings two pence was deducted from the weekly wage. Work commenced at 8.45am, thirty minutes for lunch, and work ended at 6.00pm. Wednesday was a half day and then you finished at 1.00pm. It all amounted to a 48 hour week for which I got 18 shillings and 8 pence and when dinners were deducted, this left me with 9 shillings and 6 pence to take home. Not a princely amount but standard for beginners. A seat at the cinema cost 1 shilling and 4 pence and if you could persuade your favourite young lady to accompany you, you could have a wonderful time in the back seat of the Colosseum for half a crown. The bar of chocolate you bought was only two pence.

The wages were small and the hours long, but if you finished your tasks early you could warm your hands at the only source of heat at work – an anthracite stove. This was at the back of the grocery department. However, Bernie Murphy, another "slag" and I decided there was something else possible.

We were all keen on ballroom dancing and Bernie was an acknowledged expert. So I tried to learn the steps for him in the half-light at the far end of the warehouse when Mr MacBrateney went for his tea at 5.30pm each day. We reckoned it must have been his good eyesight or just instincts, because once he stopped on his way back. He had no intention of moving until we did. We each grabbed a case of goods to pretend we were re-stocking the shelves and boldly proceeded. He let us pass and then his nasal voice cut the air like a whip, "Come here you two," he said and drawing himself up to the full height of his six foot two inches, he peered down his nose and with his piercing eyes continued, "You need to wake up when you come in in the mornings, not when you are going home at night. Now put those goods back and don't let me catch you again or out you will go!"

Tying bags and parcels securely was essential and something to be learned correctly. Mr Mac would stand quietly behind you as you struggled to get it right, especially if it was a parcel for the post. Then he would examine what you had done to see if it would pass.

If it was not really tight and secure, he would cut the twine and demonstrate the way it should be done, finally dropping it on the counter and saying, "Now boy, that could go to America". With his height and tone you would feel about four feet high, or less. One day, such a scene involved me but at the crucial moment as he dropped the parcel onto the counter and began to speak, the string broke, so he quickly changed his sentence to, "That wouldn't go any bloody place" and stomped off leaving me trying to hold back my mirth.

Told Off

One of the most sarcastic comments which was said to me occurred one day when I happened to be sitting opposite him at lunch. I wanted a drink of water and lifting the jug politely enquired, "Water Mr Mac?" I received a withering glance and the reply, "I never drink it by itself!" He was telling the truth. Nevertheless, we all liked and respected him. He was a good buyer and his remarks were recounted again and again and provided great laughs in an otherwise rather dull job. Furthermore, he was a good friend of my father and when it came to holidays that year we were allowed off at the same time. We went to visit my sister, now married and living in Portsmouth, or Pompey in British Army parlance.

We weren't there long before my father received a telegram from John L. Musgrave himself. I was ordered to report to him immediately upon our return. We knew that in my first year we were entirely out of line taking holidays in August, prime time. Despite this, we enjoyed ourselves. There was an amusement park that my father discovered was operated by a Jewish friend from Cork and we were invited to visit their home. He had a lovely daughter and while father tried his luck at the stalls, she borrowed one of the family speedboats and off we went roaring over the

Solent. It was exhilarating fun and we never realised how danger-ous it was, as obstacles were difficult to see in the darkness of the waters and a fatal collision was always a possibility. On returning home to Cork, as instructed I reported at 8.30am to Mr John with the post, "Ah, Creighton" he said, "You are back".

"Yes, Mr John," I replied.

"Who told you to go on holiday?"

"Mr MacBrateney, Mr John"

"Your father knew full well that for you to take holiday in your first year in the month of August was entirely wrong. Now as long as you work here I will tell you when to go on holiday, under-stand?"

"Yes, Mr John," I answered, feeling very small indeed.

He kept to his word and informed me in 1928 that I could take my supposedly summer holidays the first two weeks in March! What could I do? Not to be beaten however, I arranged to spend my 14 days with one of our travellers on his journey. Jack Jenkins called on all accounts and sold everything stocked in the Fancy Room except for sweet confectionery. He drove an Austin ten hun-dred weight van full of suitcases containing samples. He and I got on famously together and I thought about how I would love to be a traveller. I helped to bring the cases in and out of the shops and it was a very slow job. Perhaps only two or three accounts could be covered in a whole day. However, the goods carried high margins, so it was worth it. Our first night was spent in a hotel in a County Waterford town. The hotel was run by Jack Tompkins, whose wife was a half twin. Her sister never married but lived with them and helped with the business. The women were almost identical and to confound things further they even dressed more or less the same. One evening a bunch of us travellers were sitting around the fire in the commercial room chatting and enjoying a night cap. Jack's wife, or was it his sister-in-law, wandered in and out.

In a quiet moment, one of the travellers said to Jack, "Tell me Jack, how the devil do you tell one of those women from the other?", Jack's face widened into a huge grin, "Never bothers me!" he said.

A few nights later we were in another hotel that was once a "great" house, and the large kitchen had a paved floor and big cupboards from floor to ceiling. One of these, strange to say, when opened out held a piano. Being well able to play, I sat down and soon the waitresses, cooks and helpers were all merrily dancing. I had no experience of strong drink, but when asked what I would like I asked for a port. The port kept coming along and I kept the music going until after midnight, but when I went to proceed upstairs to bed, I couldn't even see the stairs and fell flat on my face. I was drunk, and next morning I had a monumental hangover. I was learning the hard way.

Besides collecting the post each morning, it was also my duty to deliver the post to the General Post Office each evening. All letters had to be stamped individually by hand and it entailed one late night, usually Friday, as then things tended to peak.

There were compensations. The post table was situated in the main offices opposite the large anthracite stove that was the sole heating agent. It was also the most recent female recruit's job to do the post, and I had a very nice companion in Mary. The security man, an ex-policeman, was very accommodating. When he ascertained what time we would finish, he would lock us in and return later to leave us out. Mary and I were very good friends and both became boating enthusiasts. I had taken up the sport of rowing with Cork Boat Club and at weekends if you could get a wherry for an afternoon or evening and persuade your favourite girl to go for a spin, a very pleasant time was assured.

Sometimes, it was a foursome and on one such trip we overstayed and when we got back to the boat, the tide had dropped and the only access was through a narrow channel in the mud banks. One of us got the boat out near the main river and the other, having taken off his shoes and socks and rolled his pants as high as possible, hoisted a girl on his back and with much arguing and shouting managed to transport her to the boat. It was very late when we all got home and we lost our two young lady-friends for good.

Bill was also a member of Cork Boat Club. One evening, he and three friends went for a row across the river, under a railway and road bridge and along a tree-lined waterway to the picturesque town of Glanmire. Tying up the boat, they went for a stroll around and ended up in a pub. They emerged in good form, but it was now dark so they had a difficult job in negotiating the narrow channel to the main river as the tide had receded. They were getting on fine but there was a dreadful smell around and they commented to each other how the smell from the river was never so bad. When they finally reached the Club and electric light, they found out to their horror that it was not the river that caused the odour. Someone in Glanmire had emptied the contents of an outdoor toilet into the river, but in the dark they did not see the boat! The lads were in a dreadful mess and furthermore, the caretaker refused to clean up the boat so they had to spend a whole morning scrubbing and washing. My brother was now a commercial traveller for an animal feed company and the much envied possessor of an Austin car.

He had also married and moved out of our house; my sister was married and our two other brothers had left Cork some years previously. One had taken up work in the Grocery trade and the other joined the Army to see the world. My father and I remained on with the help of a housekeeper.

CHAPTER 7

A CHANGE OF WORK

After three years I was transferred to the Fancy Room and I liked the change. The work was different and besides compiling orders, I was responsible for incoming goods, stocking shelves, and I was now the guardian of the sweet confectionery. I vowed to stop the breaking open of boxes and sampling of sweets, but I also knew how great a craving it could be and how it was hard to smother. I therefore got permission to leave a box of our own make sweets open for all to sample. I also made known that there was to be no more pilfering. The boys were mostly the culprits and one day I caught one of them red-handed; he got a boot up the back-side, a rough hand on his neck, and a few choice words. The news went around, I had made my point and there was no more pilfering.

The Department was controlled by Miss Kathleen Sullivan on a day-to-day basis, but the Boss was Mr James Best. He lived in Sutton, Co. Dublin, and arrived by train each Tuesday and departed on Friday.

He was also a buyer and was an excellent trader and bought considerable quantities of galvanised ware and toys directly from Germany and England.

I had to get to know the full range of stock from the wide range of druggists sundries and cattle medicines, through to cosmetics and hair preparations. Much of the sweet confectionery was our own manufacture including lozenges and toffee. Then there was aluminium ware, cycle accessories, cutlery, combs, enamel ware, glasses, handkerchiefs, hosiery, laces, hurleys, lamps and burners, braces, attaché cases, tinware, feeding bottles, teats and soothers, mouse and rat traps and shirts to mention a few, all to be sorted and stocked – not to mention the wide range of toys for the Christmas trade.

I now came in much closer contact with our traveller Mr Jenkins, with whom I had spent that eventful holiday. I was responsible for keeping his samples up to date. Events were to prove that this latter activity was very valuable in advancing my ambitions.

My salary had now been increased to three pounds a week, and the apprenticeship was to last five years. Each year there was a test to pass set by Mr John L. Musgrave and if successful the wages were increased. The problem was that he was a very busy man and it could be up to six or seven weeks after an anniversary that he would inform you, without warning, to report to Miss Dearnley for the test. Like all the rest of the apprentices, I found myself in this situation. These tests included knowledge of the trade and also of the private code of figures. These were symbols for each number 1 to 10 and they had to be precisely formed so that there could be no mistakes. They had to be used exactly as ordinary figures. Their purpose was to keep the costs private and while the junior worker had not much use for them, they formed a principle component in the system and were essential, as I discovered later on. It was vital to be prepared for the annual test as most of it consisted of exercises you didn't really use on a daily basis. As you did not know exactly when you would be called, it was quite worrying. One night I had an unusual dream, I dreamt that I had been called for my test and had failed as I could not do anything correctly. I woke up in a cold sweat.

It seemed like a clear message so I brushed up on the tots and private figures. Good job too, for a week later the axe fell and I was ready. I got the test 100 per cent correct. I felt that this was time to do something about the system and that I was in a good position to start. When Mr John told me I had done well I made the point that since I had done well in all my tests that it was fruitless to have any more and to my surprise, he agreed. Many were quite afraid of the Boss whoever it was in those days – for there were no trade unions to protect the workers and the boss could hire and fire as he deemed fit. Should you lose your job, it was very hard to find another. I had no fear of people and was well able to express myself in a calm and logical manner. I know Mr John respected anyone who faced up to him, he was shrewd enough to know that I was a valuable asset that could prove useful to the firm. He was to be proved correct.

A Not So Funny Incident

My interest in music still continued and my very close friend Bill Geeve and I thought we could make a few extra pounds if we got a band going. An opening existed as parish dances were held in St Nicholas' Parochial Hall each Friday night.

We enlisted a violinist, Pat Hegarty, and Jack Redden, who played the coronet in St Nicholas' Brass Band, fitted in well as the trumpeter. We had great fun and made more money from our one-night stand then we did in six working days .

Christmas was a very busy time in Musgrave Brothers. Jimmy Best had perfected our purchase of dolls from Germany. Before he went to the toy fairs, he pre-sold in case lots to a wide range of toy retailers. His total buying order was then considerably enhanced. Dolls retailed at one shilling, half a crown (two shillings and six pence) five shillings and ten shillings. They were shipped in huge timber cases measuring six by four by eight feet and had to be unpacked and the contents stored on shelves. It went on for days non-stop. We were worked to exhaustion. Jimmy Best, besides being a good buyer, was a bit of a slave driver and he had command of some strong language which he directed at me and my fellow workers. He would sit on a box and order us to greater effort all day long. The second year I was involved, I felt something had to be done to stop this treatment.

James Best usually had a light lunch of sandwiches or sometimes sent me across the street for cooked pig "crubeens", of which he was very fond. I also had to make him a cup of tea, getting the tea from the Tea Department. On one occasion, I had the dreadful idea of putting something into the tea to keep him occupied all day – a whole packet of Beechams Pills for instance! No sooner thought than the dreadful deed was done. We did not see sight nor sign of him for the rest of the day and the next day he was to go off to Dublin, though not before he hauled me over knowing I had put something in his tea. "Where did you get the tea Arthur?" he thundered. "From Mr Wilkie, Mr Best. It was the best tea in the house." "Bloody awful taste. What did you put into it?" Getting nowhere, he told me to get out of his sight before he lost his temper, so I did. Two years later I was having dinner with him at Miss Sullivan's house – where he lodged when in Cork. Over coffee and a cigarette afterwards he asked, "Tell me what you put into the tea that day." And as I knew him and Miss Sullivan very well by then, I told him. He burst out laughing and told me he had never felt so good as he had for several weeks after that episode.

First Taste of Selling

James Best had another job besides managing the Fancy Department as he had the agency to sell Musgrave manufactured sweets to the wholesale trade. The factory was on the Quay at the rear of the Metropole Hotel and was under the control of Mr Stuart Musgrave. We offered a wide range of count lines at a penny and half a penny each, good old Peggies Leg, mixed rock – including brown, pineapple, peppermint, raspberry and Tipperary; Money Balls, a great favourite as within the pink lumps of sugar you might find a real half-penny. We also made barley sugar and Peggies Toes and assorted toffees for only half a penny. Remember, I now got three pounds a week – 720 pennies – for a whole week's work, but look what a half penny could buy a child if he got six pence a week pocket-money! We manufactured boiled sweets packed in free twenty-eight pound galvanised buckets, seven pound cans and four pound bottles. There were the old reliables, Bull's Eyes, Clove Balls, Acid Drops, Brown Cushions, Butterscotch, Pear Drops and

Brandy Balls etc., and also boiled sweets in twenty-four varieties, including butter nuggets, bramble berry, and butterscotch, with Metropole Mixture being the most popular. The assorted toffees came in five different varieties.

We manufactured Edinburgh Rock, Hore Hound candy for colds, Rum & Butter bon-bons at sixteen for a penny, Butter Mints and Fruit Drops. We did a very fine business in Peppermint Lozenges, which were sold in a four penny size – the same size as the old four penny piece by then withdrawn, a six penny thick mint size, and also a shilling thick mint. The names only applied to the size not to the price as they sold at either twelve, sixteen or thirty-six lozenges for a penny! Other lozenges sold were Musk Lozenges, Winter Lozenges, Extra Strong and LL & C – liquorice, linseed and chlordyne for colds and there were Sherbet Fountains and other sherbet lines. So, we had a very fine range.

James Best thought that I was the bright boy who could help him during the three busy days he spent in Cork. I got the job of calling to the wholesale accounts once a week. He would only then have to call once a month. This was my first attempt at selling anything and I had no training, but I had a quick and voluble tongue, could think quickly and intelligently, and was good with figures. I also had a pleasant manner.

The men I called on were mostly old enough to be my father and owned their own businesses. They distributed by van and often also handled fruit. I really did not have an opportunity to sell anything as the men knew what was in stock and simply ordered whatever was short. I did feel very much like the small boy, especially as I was frequently addressed as the "Young Fellow from Musgraves". To add to the problem I was only five foot six inches although I was twenty years old and well built, I looked younger and had fair hair, blue eyes and a good complexion. Therefore, I decided to grow a moustache thinking it should help. I did, and it has remained ever since! I do not know if it increased the sale of the sweets, but I got a lot of "ragging" over it and this only strengthened my determination not to shave it off. Then, during a holiday with my father in Portsmouth, I admired a pipe in a shop window and he said, "If you like it then buy it," so I did. The pipe was a bent-shape style and I smoked some of my father's tobacco but it made me feel sick. At first, I could only smoke before retiring at night so that I could then lie down! Like the "tash", this also was the cause of many jokes especially when I produced the pipe in the tiny smoke room in Musgraves (it was only twelve by ten feet for staff of thirty men and boys). The usual comment was, "Where is the pipe going with the small boy?" so I was determined to persist all the more.

Another job I had was arranged between Tom MacBrateney, James Best and my father. This was to calculate all the stock after stock-taking. I was closeted in a small office for days and days. Stock-taking was a huge job as all shelves had to be tidied and we had to try and get the orders on hand away quickly. Once that was done, stock-taking would begin and would continue until it was finished. This meant working late into the night. The only customers who were attended to were callers, and these sales had to be added to the stock. Should the stock ever be wrong, we would have to start again. However, we got one-and-a-quarter our usual rate for working overtime. The extra money was handy and made up for the longer hours. One thing the stock-taking did for me was to keep my brain sharp for figures. My father was a great help here as he had innumerable quick methods of calculation and all this stood to me in the future.

Another event occurred when there was a 'flu epidemic and only one of our travellers was able to carry on working. This was the same Carl Humphries now promoted and he suggested that I should be "lent" to him and he would see what he could do with me! We set off in his Morris Cowley car for Blackpool. I had never been to the north side of the City before and he stopped by Blackpool Bridge and said "Look, there is Commons Road, Watercourse Road, Thomas Davis Street and that is Gerald Griffen Street. Over there is your first call, I will meet you here at one."

I was quite taken aback but off I went clutching a bag containing accounts to be called on and an order book, as I heard Carl shouting, "Have you a pencil?". I found my way along and customers were helpful and I met Carl again as agreed for lunch. After a week of all this I developed laryngitis, but John L. came to the rescue. He lent me an apparatus that looked like a perfume atomizer but contained an oily creosote smelling liquid that was sprayed down the throat and helped immediately. It was very funny as I would march into a shop, smile at the person behind the counter and then spray my throat so that I could speak clearly – I got lots of laughs but was learning all the time.

In my free time I was still keen on rowing and was selected to row in the Cork City Regatta for the under-21 team of eight in 1932. However, I had a problem. As fine a business man as John L. was, he had no time for sport and I had to make special arrangements for a day off. This, of course, also involved my father and James Best. All went well, we did not win but did acquit ourselves credibly.

It's an Ill Wind

In September of that year another opportunity arrived for me to sample life "on the road". My old friend, Jack Jenkins, had injured his back and slipped a disk by pulling too hard on the car's handbrake to avoid a hitting a child at Chapelgate in Rathmore. He was unable to drive. Another one of the staff, Jim Robinson, suggested that he would take over the job if I would accompany him as I knew the Fancy Room's range of goods. Off we both set in the Austin ten hundred weight van packed to the door with samples in suitcases. No suitcase was labelled as Jack knew the cases and what was in each. Our first call was to Ardmore in County Waterford where there was a very good customer, certainly one of the most good natured I had ever met. She sat patiently while I carried every case in from the van as we did not know what was in them until they were open.

She saw so much that I am sure we sold her three or six of each – almost half our entire range! After that we felt more at ease. Jim Robinson had one of the most pleasing manners of anyone I ever met. We spent four weeks together and I thoroughly enjoyed every minute. By then Jack Jenkins was much better but still unable to drive. As I now had some experience of driving my brothers Austin and also had Jim Robinson's tuition as the vehicles were similar, I set off travelling again.

Austins, in common with all cars then, had a gear changing device called a "gate change", which was shaped like the letter "H" with a side attachment for reverse. Top left was first gear, bottom left was second, the middle was neutral, top right was third and bottom right was forth. To get the car to reverse the gear stick had to be at the neutral position, then pulled over to the right and down. It took a lot of effort as there was only one notch for each gear that the gear stick would go into and it would not just slide into position. Quite complicated it sounds and quite complicated it was, as to preform a change without a dreadful grating noise you had to push out the clutch, draw the lever back midway (neutral) give the accelerator a dart and push the lever into the new gear.

I got the hang of it but it involved a lot of practise, especially when changing down through the gears as the car climbed up a hill. Then you had to push down longer on the accelerator to make a smooth change.

Jack Jenkins and I set off for the Cork and Kerry border one damp and dismal Monday morning. The main road was alright but then we got on to the by-roads and these were a sea of mud. It was not easy to keep the little van on the road. Jack did not say one word of reproach as we skidded along on either side of the road, but I am sure his heart was in his mouth – mine was. As it was approaching Christmas, we had a huge range of toys and due to his illness there were many calls to make. We had to work from 9.30am to 9.30pm every day, usually away from towns so we had to make do with our customers' hospitality. It was a good thing that we were both capable of eating boiled eggs and home-made bastible bread day after day for lunch.

Bastible bread was made in a metal pot that hung over a turf fire. Hot turf was also placed on the lid of the pot to surround the bread with heat. The resulting bread was a flat round loaf about two or three inches high with a lovely nutty flavour. Alas, it is no longer baked. If you were lucky you would get home-made dairy butter and the combination was a delight.

I well remember my very first night with Jack Jenkins at the "Baron's" house, where he and his wife ran a pub and kept guests, in Knocknagree. That night was remarkable as his wife had grilled lovely lamb chops on hot bars over the turf fire – absolutely delicious. I ate and ate and in the morning Jack told me that I had eaten over a dozen chops! The "Baron" got his name because he had the right to collect a headage payment on each animal sold at the local cattle fair. That was the one day that the travellers avoided, as the owners of the shops and pubs were too busy to do any buying. It was selling only on that day. The farmers sold the cattle and had a few drinks while the women had a shopping spree. Knocknagree village is perched up on a hill near Rathmore and it could get very wild as the wind roared up over the bog valley from Killarney.

At the end of our first week we visited a customer on the hill near the square. It was dark, wet and very windy. I was handing the cases in and out of the van but as I was packing them into the van I was sure that I was missing one. I told Jack and he thought I was mistaken and must have packed it in already without noticing it. The following day however, it appeared that Christmas had come early for the children as they trudged up the hill to school. Much to their surprise and delight there were toys scattered all along the road side. The wind must have blown the case away and all we could recover was the battered case!

Jack and I continued selling until Christmas and I became a good careful driver. I knew lots more about selling as Jack Jenkins quietly passed on valuable tips of the trade and I was a very apt pupil. He was a very astute observer of human nature and taught me to recognise that each individual was different. To successfully sell to them it was necessary to know all you could about their likes and dislikes, mannerisms and family background and to memorise all this information. What a teacher!

Jack Jenkins was also a good friend and fond of music. I was often invited to his home for tea and a musical evening when his two attractive daughters and I would play and sing his favourite arias.

Usually for a night out we went to the dances at the Gregg Hall in the Grand Parade (home of the Church of Ireland Young Men's Association), the A.O.H. Hall in Queen's Street or St Nicholas' in Cove Street. On special occasions we went to the Arcadia Ballroom – opposite the Railway Station on the Lower Road. We had lots of girlfriends but no cars so we had to take the trams or walk, but we did not worry about much else but whom we may have the pleasure of walking home with after the dance. There was a great sense of adventure about it all.

Cycling was another enjoyable pastime and we would cycle anywhere. After work, an evening spin to Crosshaven if the weather was kind enough for a swim was great. My pals, Bill Geeve, Bill Hanna, Harold Good and I often went to Youghal or Ballycotton as well. It was Bill Geeve and I, however, who were the fanatics and a trip to the Old Head of Kinsale and home through Innishannon, about 60 miles, was no trouble to us then.

I remember also going to Fermoy and back in one afternoon just so he could see his sweetheart, Edie Glouster. She had tragically lost her father, a member of the Royal Irish Constabulary, who, along with his comrades, was blown up by an IRA bomb thrown into their vehicle at Barrack's Street in 1921.

CHAPTER 8

ON THE ROAD

In 1933, John Barry who was the Fancy Room's town traveller was leaving Musgrave Brothers to join Punch & Company (one of the main opposition companies). This provided an opening for a new person and there I was raring to go, with some experience in the trade and a knowledge of how to sell – now my time had come.

John L. Musgrave was a shrewd business man and his system was quite a masterpiece of incentive, coupled with real profit not turnover. It began with the buyers, as they bought at the best price they could negotiate in the market place and sold for the best price they could get. Once cost prices and approximate handling charges were established, the selling price was set. This was largely what the Buyer calculated the market could stand for each product but, he had to show a profit of between 10 per cent and 16.66 per cent from the original cost price.

The Buyer then recorded the difference between the cost including handling and the original cost, this could be a penny or more per item, on each sales invoice. The difference was small but at the year-end this was given as an extra bonus and could then be £200 or £300. It was easier to obtain on imported goods, bulk goods bought on world markets – such as dried fruit, or bulk cereals, rice, tapioca, etc., bought through agents. There was little room for extra profit on standard brand manufactured lines however. Once the house cost was established, it was then entered by all who had need to use a cost book. This meant the travellers, and the private figures mentioned previously were always used. Therefore, if a book got mislaid it would be of no use to anyone, particularly the opposition, if they found it.

Each traveller had a cost book that was leather bound with very good quality paper and euphemistically called "The Bible". The paper had to be good quality as prices were changed frequently, always in pencil, so there was a lot of erasing. A weekly price change list was produced so that the books were up to date at all times. All items sold were handwritten into large day books, some were fifteen inches long by ten inches wide and five inches deep, so they were very heavy.

The selling prices were in pounds, shillings and pence, (two farthings equalled a half-penny, twelve pennies made a shilling and twenty shillings made a pound). There was a selling price column in which all sales were calculated and a blank column. The cost price was calculated and entered in the blank column by the traveller if he happened to be in town at the time. All invoices were totted to give the total week's sales and the cost prices were totalled also – the difference being the weekly profit. Each traveller got a commission of one per cent on any profit he made in excess of what was made the previous year. This commission was paid at the year-end. He also got an extra commission on tea and factory goods. For tea, this was one farthing on every pound sold and as tea was sold in five or ten pound bags and fifty or one hundred pound chests the chance of commission was high, the sale of a chest of tea provided twenty-five pence commission. Factory sales were calculated in hundredweights and the commission was three pence per hundredweight. All very complicated and labour intensive but John L. knew what was happening on a weekly basis. This was something very few, if any, of his competitors did. There was also a ten shilling bonus for any new accounts opened provided that they were still trading at the end of twelve months.

A traveller had plenty to aim for and profit, not turnover, was the goal. Consequently, if he was wise he would try to sell items with high margins and this was where the Fancy Room featured as margins could be much higher than on food items. Sugar, in which we did a large trade, gave the worst profit of all even though we would import a whole cargo together with an opposition company

Newsom & Sons of French Church Street. Sugar was costing eighteen shillings and eight pence for a hundredweight which is two pence a pound, and sold at two and a half pence a pound – a very small margin.

My new job was to call on all operating accounts already covered by Carl Humphries and Abe Huggard and to sell all lines carried by the Fancy Room except Confectionery. I was also free to open any new accounts that I could get and to these I could sell any items in stock as they would be wholly my accounts. It was a definite challenge. Carl's territory was the area south of the River Lee and Crosshaven, while Abe's was north of the River and Queenstown (Cobh). Orders for the city areas were compiled by different staff in different parts of the warehouse from the country orders and this was called the "town department".

The man in charge was William (Billy) Locke and we were fortunate to have such a fine "boss". He was as straight as a die and a strict disciplinarian, but with a great personality and a born leader. He kept us all on our toes but he made people feel appreciated and I benefitted immensely from his example. One meets many fine people travelling through life and Billy Locke was in the top bracket of that elite. From those early days we became lifelong friends, unfortunately he is no longer with us.

Street Scenes and I Put my Foot in it

Like all local travellers, I had to report at 9.45am with the previous afternoon's orders and cash, then do a half an hour or so costing my previous orders, and then set off on the day's selling. I began travelling by bicycle all over Cork City and soon knew every lane and alley both north and south of the river – from Blackpool, Shandon Street, Fairhill, Kerry Pike Lane, North Main Street, The Marsh, St. Luke's and Mayfield on the north side to Barrack's Street, The Lough, Magazine Road and College Road on the south side and everywhere in between. The city centre was dominated by the bigger grocery retailers, Woodford Bourne, Allcock, Home &

Colonial, Lipton's, and Smith's Stores.

Only Home & Colonial and Lipton's sold for cash or priced goods. Credit was widespread and all large orders were delivered to the home or institution. I also called to traders on the street where Musgrave Brothers was, Cornmarket Street, known as The Coal Quay as that was its purpose until it was filled in and made part of the main central island on which Cork City rests. All one side of the street used to be dominated by street stalls selling vegetables, fish, second-hand clothes, pig offal, fruit, and many other odds and ends. The female operators of these stall were nicknamed "Shawly Mags" as they wore the old-fashioned dress of a black skirt, dark pullover and a dark shawl.

These women had a reputation for having sharp tongues and flowery vocabulary but I did business with many of them and they were good honest business women who enjoyed a bit of "craic". One morning as I was about to go off on my bicycle, I saw a great commotion in the street. On getting closer, I saw two of these "ladies" engaged in a huge fight, screeching obscenities at each other, scratching faces and pulling out hair. This was being watched by a gathering crowd.

I had work to do and could not delay but on my way back for my midday meal, there they were sitting on the pavement, friends again, with the blood on their faces hardly dry. As I passed I heard the comment, "You know, it wasn't what you called me Mags, but the dirty rotten way that you said it!"

There are some things one learns the hard way, and it is by no means the worst way to learn. One of the most competitive areas of the business was dried fruit, imported from Greece, Turkey and California. Samples were carried in little boxes and generally, the lighter in colour sultanas were, the more expensive they were.

Once I was doing my best to get an order that could have been for a few hundredweight (say ten 30lb boxes) of dried fruit but my quote was too high. The customer, with whom I was on very good terms, ran a very well kept shop in Barrack's Street and was one of the up and coming breed of retailers who sold for cash at low prices – no credit whatsoever. She showed me a scoop of her lowest priced sultanas that she was selling at a price nearly as low as I was offering wholesale but the quality was poorer. Unfortunately, I then committed a fatal error and one that I was to regret.

I said, "Yes, Mrs Dempsey, they are not the greatest but they certainly are cheap." She turned a fiery red colour as I had hurt her pride and her temper flared. "Young man," she thundered, "there is nothing cheap about this shop or anything in it, now go and sell your fruit elsewhere." I had enough common sense not to push my case any further while she was in such a mood, so I left quietly but very upset that I had lost a good order if not a whole account. I knew that if I came up with a good quote it might help her to change her mind. The house rule was that no goods, except sugar, could be sold at less than 10 per cent profit, but margins were better on tea so here there was more leeway. I had a talk with Tom MacBrateney, who helped me out with a few good lines in rice at the best prices and Alan Wilkie blended a tea for me that cost only one shilling a pound. Thus armed, I was able to face the lady again the following week. I chose a quiet time to call as I did not want any interruptions and in I went. I apologised for the previous week's upset and hoped that she would forgive me. She stated that she was hurt about the insult which I had made to her shop. Having stressed that she had one of the cleanest and neatest shops in the city I was eventually forgiven.

I knew now that to seal over the crack in our otherwise good relations that I would have to sell her something and get the account open again, the rice and tea did the trick, but I would never use the word "cheap" again, instead it would be low cost, low priced, or inexpensive.

The Hard Slog

Our official half-day was on Wednesday, but for travellers there was no official half-day. Regular journeys were carried out on weekdays

THE LIFE AND TIMES OF ARTHUR HENRY

and, on Friday night, if the costing was not completed, you would have to drag the heavy book home because it had to be up to date by Saturday morning, hail, rain or shine. However, my book was not very big at that time. Mr. Musgrave interviewed every traveller on a weekly basis and went over each account for the coming week. Credit was widespread and our terms were 3.75 per cent for one month, 2.5 per cent for two months and 1.25 per cent for three months. After that, strictly nett.

The credit-worthiness of an account rested very much with the traveller, although we did get private reports from an agency. Invariably, some accounts did go wrong and had to be collected, very often on an agreed reduction of as little as ten shillings every week. Collecting these got me into some unusual places as when a shop went bankrupt, the owners often had to move to much poorer quarters maybe just a rented room for a whole family. Two houses in particular stand out in my memory. One was in Cattlemarket Street, off Shandon Street. In this one house, twenty families were trying to exist. The other was in an area known as The Marsh, now Gratten Street. It was a Queen Ann period square building with steps leading to the pointed top entrance and was commonly called The Doll's House. It accommodated, if that is the correct word, no less than thirty families. They all looked after each other and one saucepan or kettle often did several families. They all knew what it was like not to have the essentials.

Often while waiting in a shop for a customer to be free to do business with me (a time consuming problem), I would overhear and wonder about the shopping lists being filled. In one shop a common request was for only a half-quarter of butter, quarter-pound of sugar, half a loaf of bread and one ounce of tea. I was intrigued and when I finally picked up the courage to enquire about the order, I was amazed to learn that the same order was repeated three times every day. It was the misfortunate woman's way of feeding her family as no matter how much was put on the table for each meal, they ate it all there and then. Shopping three times a day ensured enough food for each of the three meals. Times were hard for many and social services were non-existent.

Cupid's Arrow Finds its Mark

In 1935, events that were to change my life forever and much for the better began to evolve.

I was still keen on the St Nicholas Friday night "hop", for we had disbanded the band, some said it was for the sake of better music as we were replaced by professionals who were much better and also much more expensive. It now cost two shillings and six pence for the night. I had the job of escorting a neighbour's daughter, Peggy, each Friday night and whilst she was a very nice girl, I felt that her mother had other designs for me rather than just an escort for the dance.

One evening Peggy decided to call for a friend on the way and then I was introduced to Gladys. Here was someone quiet different. We had several dances, including the last, and I escorted them both home. This repeated itself the following week and then Peggy said she could not go because she was invited to a party. Instead I just called for Gladys and we also made a date to go to a film that Wednesday. At that time I had a lots of interests, I was still in the brass band and I had another beautiful dancing partner that I took to the Arcadia on Thursdays, and was also interested in an American girl. Gladys had badminton on Tuesday and Thursday evening and I had to work Fridays but, we met each other in between. Summer came and our romance fizzled out as I was busy cycling and swimming but when autumn came I thought about Gladys again. She was a supervisor in a glove manufacturing company with premises in Patrick's Street and one day I boldly marched in and asked to see her. She was in no way beholden to me, and was busy as a big order had to be sent out and, more to get rid of me than any other reason, she agreed to meet me the following evening and go to the Pavilion Picture House where a good film was showing.

We met at the old meeting place and when I saw her coming towards me, my heart gave a jump. She had a smart walk and a bright smile and I knew this girl was different. From then on there was no turning back. The more we saw of one another the more I realised how I had nearly missed her. I was hooked and I loved it.

My friend, Bill Geeve, was still very much in love with Edie, and the two girls got on well. We had great picnics most Sundays (the only day off) and we would cycle to Robert's Cove or more often to Kinsale, where we had a special cove to ourselves.

The fact that this meant pushing the bicycle past Charles Fort, over a stream and down by a cliff did not put us off and our main thought was to have the two ladies to ourselves for the whole afternoon and that was really wonderful. They were great days and we made the most of them.

One Last Adventure

The previous year Bill and I had visited an aunt of his, a widow, who lived in Pollockshaws, Glasgow. Her son, David Bishop, conducted us through the tougher parts of the city where police had to patrol in pairs. He had friends there who lived in a council flat and here we saw something we had never seen before: a double bed that could fold up into a recess in the wall during the day, so the one room served as a living room and a bedroom. One of David's friends, Jim, had an ugly scar running down his cheek, the nasty hallmark of being a member of a street gang. One evening his sister had answered a knock on the front door and a young man enquired if her brother was in. She said that he was and called him, but when Jim reached the door the other man made a quick swipe at him with a knife and shouted, "Ask your sister to stitch that up", and ran off. Such was life in the tough quarters of that great city, but we loved Glasgow and we got on very well with Mrs Bishop.

In the summer of 1935 Bill and I planned to go on a cruise – just the two of us as a last bachelor fling as it were. Bill was a great organiser and arranged the trip. We sailed from Tilbury to

Hamburg, through the Kiel Canal and onto Copenhagen. Ship life was great fun and we met up with two very charming young ladies. Copenhagen was a new experience for us, our first visit to a European capital, and we admired the very fine buildings, the ship crowded harbour, the lovely walk along the Langalinie to see the famous bronze mermaid and of course the fantastic Tivoli Gardens Fun Fair. We also paid a memorable visit to the Carlsberg Brewery and got mixed up with a party of huge Danish farmers, so we all drank far too much of the free lager and suffered afterwards for it. The next port of call was Oslo, another quite different experience.

Here, one of the two ladies, Dorothy, and I were looking for the Norfolk Museum and getting totally lost. We enquired of a passing stranger who replied that he was also seeking the same place. His name was William Sward from Sweden. We walked along together until we came upon some workmen who were digging up the road, and he asked directions in their own language. We found the museum and had a lovely meal that evening in one of the many restaurants situated on the islands in the harbour. Before parting, William and I exchanged addresses and thereby started a friendship that lasted a lifetime. Our last port of call was Kristiansund, a small port at the end of a fjord. The weather was great so we went for a swim. Bill and I, and our two young lady friends, set off further along the shore. As we togged off we noticed a strange structure on the opposite shore, like a grandstand that you would see at a football game, but it sloped down to the water. As we swam towards it we got a better view. There was a dividing partition and one side was very obviously for men and the other for women. They were all sunning themselves absolutely naked. We had never heard about the Scandinavians love of the free life. The term "nudist colony" had not even been coined then. We just could not comprehend this at all and we were somewhat embarrassed. Bill and I knew that we would never be able to relate the story at home because nobody would believe us in Ireland so we decided to try and forget all about it.

When back in Cork once more we found Edie and Gladys to be extraordinarily understanding about our trip. We were all very confident about our respective relationships.We knew they were to last.

Of Dress and Mess

Business was considered to be by far the most important aspect in life and proper business dress was essential, a dark suit with a white shirt, a tie, and black well polished shoes. One morning in the Fancy room I was present when a traveller from Barker & Dobson, the English confectionery manufacturers, called to see James Best. Usually he would be attired in the conventional manner and often sported a pink rose in his button-hole, but this day he was taking the morning off to play golf and was wearing his golfing apparel of brown boots, long stockings, and baggy knickerbockers called plus fours.

"Good morning James," said the traveller. "I am on my way to the Island and just called for my order as I was passing."

James was not in good form, and didn't even greet him but said: "Where the hell do you think you are going dressed like that? If you want to do business here come properly dressed for business." He turned away and left the traveller standing.

I also witnessed quite a different episode one evening involving the same kind of attire at Cork Boat Club. There were two brothers, surnamed Brown, one was a strong powerful chap who took his rowing seriously and was in the senior eight, the other didn't row much but liked to cox, and that evening he was also attired in plus fours. Evidently, on the river he had been pushing the lads hard, especially his brother. Now when any boat pulled into the slip there was a standard procedure. The boatman held an outrigger and the bow oarsman stepped out first, stood his oar against the wall, and then held the bow outrigger until each oarsman got out, the cox being last. This time however, once the eight had stepped ashore, the oarsmen who happened to be the "rowing" Brown let go and the boat capsized toppling the cox out into the muddy water.

You should have seen him wading ashore with the mud up to his knees and his baggy plus fours pouring water! The brothers didn't speak to one another for at least a week after that episode.

A Good Reason To Get a Car

My life went on as usual. I saw as much of Gladys as I could and I continued selling as much as I could on my bicycle but getting awfully wet on occasions. It was not surprising then that one morning I could not get out of bed because of the pain in my back. I called the doctor and I was sure that I had some dreadful complaint and was already imagining myself on the operating table. My doctor was a rather gruff individual and when he called he took my pulse, ordered me to sit up and then pulled me up. I roared and fell back onto the bed. "Lumbago," he said, and walked out of the room. I got over the lumbago but decided not to risk any more wettings and decided I would have to get a car. The major problem with getting a car was that my expenses were nine shillings a week and this would not run a car. I had quite a problem getting John L. to increase this to thirty shillings as he was a good man at keeping costs as low as possible. My first car was a second-hand six cylinder blue Wolseley costing sixty pounds. Shortly after that my garage-man friend, Chris O'Mahony, told me about a lovely nine horse power green Wolseley belonging to a doctor.

He said that it would shortly be coming on the market and promised he could hold it for me and he did. For the second car I traded in the first car and paid thirty pounds extra. Nowadays that would seem to be very inexpensive but it was quite a lot to put together. A driving licence cost five shillings and petrol was one shilling and two pence per gallon – the good old days! I was over the moon at having a car and a girl of my own; life was very good. It was just as well that I bought the car as shortly afterwards Abe Huggard left the company and I took over his journey. I was now a fully fledged commercial traveller with my own area – consisting of all the north side of Cork City, including Queenstown, and I was able to sell our full range. Times change and this range was quite different to what would be sold or required by people today.

As mentioned already, few lines were packed in small outers and many items are quite unfamiliar now. Some of these would include Bath Brick, which was a coarse brick for cleaning knives, Blacking for polishing fire grates and stoves, Bottled Coffee Essence (instant coffee powder was years ahead), Straw Hat Dyes, Puff Seeded Muscats in twenty-five-pound timber boxes and twenty-eight pound buckets of dripping!

There was also Poultry Spice, Pig Powder, a wide range of meat and fish pastes with fancy labels – lobster, salmon and shrimp, game, tongue and chicken, Gentlemen's Relish and American lard in twenty-eight one-pound boxes. Castor oil came in one, two, three, four, six, eight, ten, twelve, sixteen, eighteen and twenty-ounce bottles, there was also twenty ounce cattle castor oil and raw linseed oil and cod liver oil. Saltpeter was used for preserving pig-meat and senna leaves to keep your "innards" right. There was a wide range of bars of soap in half hundredweight and one hundred cases, and three penny and four and a half penny tablets including such makes as the famous Sunlight and Lifebuoy, a concoction called Monkey Brand – a coarse soap block for grimy hands, and a limited range of soap powders including Rinso and Lux in three and a half pence and seven pence packets. Starch was a big seller in quarter, half and one pound boxes, sold in half hundred and one hundred timber cases! Caraway seeds were also a big seller and they were sold in one hundredweight bags no less, as caraway seeds were put into all kinds of bread then. We sold various bird seeds including canary, rape and hemp. Treacle was a big seller and there were wax tapers for lighting candles and waterglass for preserving eggs – just a few of the oddities!

Many brand names are as well known today as they were then, such as Royal baking powder, Heinz beans, Jacob's biscuits, Coleman's mustard, Bovril, Fry's cocoa, Bird's custard, Player & Wills cigarettes and Crosse & Blackwell items. Also, Ovaltine,

Kellogg's Cornflakes and All-Bran (the large product range today was yet to be created), Jeye's Fluid, Chiver's jams, Oxo Cubes packed in sixes in a handy little tin, Friendly matches and Stork margarine, not forgetting the wide range of Spratt's specialities for birds and dogs. It is interesting to note that all cheese was imported. Eighty pound rounds of cheddar from Canada and half, one pound and five pound Kraft from the USA, most others were manufactured in England. The confectionery trade was as different as chalk is from cheese, loose boiled sweets were a huge seller and a very large trade was done in count lines. Turkish Delight, Flake and Walnuts came from Cadburys and Frys had a much larger range starting with penny bars in cream, milk or plain chocolate and going up to half-pound or one pound boxes of chocolates. Cadburys and Frys were later to merge. Rowntrees were also in production with a similar range but with the addition of two penny and six penny gums pastilles.

Compare that to the enormous variety of bars and producers of today's chocolate range.

We Defy Tradition

In 1936, Gladys and I arranged an unheard of expedition – we were going on holidays together and we were not even engaged to be married! In the strictly chaperoned young ladies world this just was not done. But all was right and proper as we were going to Glasgow to stay with Bill Geeve's aunt, Mrs Bishop, with whom I had stayed before. To get to Glasgow, one could go via the Clyde Shipping Company's steamer directly from Cork as Bill and I had done two years previously, but Gladys and I went to Dublin by train and then by boat to Glasgow. When Bill and I sailed up the Clyde in 1934 you could hardly hear with the noise of rivets being driven into the many ships under construction but by 1936 it was much quieter – the big recession had begun. We had a lovely holiday and explored the beautiful lower Clyde and the magnificent Loch Lomond up as far as Ardluie. We spent a few days in

Edinburgh, the beautiful city of Scottish kings and queens and the wonderful Edinburgh castle. We went to several good variety shows and enjoyed the Scottish humour.

By now Gladys and I had both arrived at the conclusion that life would not be the same unless we shared it. So, though we had not announced this to the world or even our parents, I bought Gladys her engagement ring in Glasgow – three diamonds set slightly off centre in white gold. On our return, in proper fashion, I asked her parents for their only daughter's hand in marriage, which came as no surprise and was readily granted.

My father and I had remained on in our house with the help of housekeepers but this was not very satisfactory and my father moved away to live with my cousins. I had kept up the rent on the house as it was in a nice locality with three good bedrooms, a nice garden and better still, the rent was under two pounds a week. So, Gladys and I would continue to live there after our wedding.

We had intended to marry the following September and were busy decorating the house while I lived there alone. However, we decided not to wait and brought the wedding forward. Thus it was that on the 16 April 1937, that Gladys Storey and Arthur Creighton were made man and wife in St John's Church, Infirmary Road, Cork. By a strange coincidence that day was also my brother Bill's birthday but, stranger still, he was married five years earlier on the 29 July – my birthday! My friend Bill Geeve was best man and Gladys' bridesmaid was her close friend Alice Coombes, a nurse in the nearby Victoria Hospital. Our honeymoon was arranged for the Channel Islands. To get there we had to take the *M/V Innisfallen* to Fishguard, a train to Bristol – arriving in time for breakfast, and after about a four-hour delay we took a train to Weymouth to board the steamer for St Helier in Jersey. Small wonder the steward had to wake us to tell us we had already berthed and to please go ashore. We stayed in the Aberfeldy Hotel and met up with an English couple, Vernon and Violet Archer, who quickly discovered it was our honeymoon when I opened my tobacco pouch and almost filled my pipe with confetti. They were on their second honeymoon having been married a year earlier. Our friendship with them has lasted our lifetime.

We were blessed with very good weather and actually walked around the island. One morning we took a bus to Gorey and walked across a hill top path to Rozell Bay. We then took a bus back to St Helier. The next day we took the bus to Rozell Bay and walked to Bouley Bay and Bonne Nuit Bay, then on to Corbiere Lighthouse and along through St Aubins and back to St Helier. It was really a wonderful experience. There was dancing in the hotel every other evening and on one such evening before dinner we were having a drink in the bar when François, a French barman, was lining up a row of cocktails along the bar counter. He had been trying to make a red, white and blue cocktail but had not succeeded, so he told us we could help ourselves to the drinks for free. We tried a few and went on to dinner and the dance. But two Welsh brothers stayed behind tasting the cocktails. Coming from the dance floor to our bedroom much later, we passed an open bedroom door – the Welsh boys – one was stretched out across his bed and the other was on the floor. Both were out for the count!

We came back to the real world with a bump on our return and began settling into our new way of life.

Evolution

Cork was a rapidly changing city. The trams ceased to run on 30 September 1931 worn out, obsolete and an obstacle to the increasingly large army of motor cars. A public transport service was developed by a man called Smith from London who inaugurated Irish Omnibus Co. in October of that year. The omnibus services were taken over by Great Southern Railway in May 1934. The horse and cart was still used and there were a few horse-drawn drays in Musgrave Brothers who by now had a fleet of lorries.

All this had a big effect on the smaller railways, the Cork to Blackrock and Passage West routes were closed and so was the

Muskerry Tram. The jaunting car, however, still fought it out with the odd taxi.

The bigger grocers, including Musgrave Brothers, Smith's Stores, L & N, Liptons, and some of the privately owned grocers still did a good business in the city centre. The suburbs were served by a huge array of smaller shops. They were our main sources for sales. My job had changed considerably as I could now carry more samples and these were essential as the job was to sell. Some of the travellers were quite careless in this regards and would boast that their words drew the picture of the product. But not me; I believed in the real thing and changed my confectionery samples weekly as new lines were always a good sell, I also carried a good range of tea samples, dried fruit and found that I could fit in higher margins on lines such as combs, hair-slides, bobby-pins, curlers and seasonal seaside lines such as balls, hurling sticks, toy tennis racquets, buckets and spades. Of course, the dreaded ledger to be costed every week was getting much bigger and Friday nights were pure torture. It was very often midnight before I could stagger into bed.

I often envied one man that was in the office, Joe Humphries, who was no relation to my colleague Carl. He had an extraordinary talent of being able to run his finger down the whole fifteen inches of a day book and within minutes write down the total answer to the tot, taking all the pounds, shillings and pence in his stride. Such concentration was unique. John L. Musgrave and my father were good at totting but they had to add the pounds, shillings and pence individually and write down each tot. There was a standing bet of five pounds to anyone who could find one of Joe's tots to be incorrect – it was never won!

I was now in the warehouse only in the mornings and was fast losing touch of the local gossip. However, one remarkable event forever stayed in my mind and I called it The True Love Story. One of the staff, Stan, was doing a strong line with a very attractive young lady and knowing that we would be working until 7.45pm

one evening, made an appointment to meet her on the quay opposite the Opera House at 8.00pm. He was there as Shandon's clock
tolled the hour. 8.15pm tolled out and no girl appeared but he still
waited. 8.30pm followed and just then he saw the familiar figure, in
a great hurry, turn down the quay from Patrick's Bridge. She
approached with great agitation and said, "Oh Stan, I am so sorry
but I was reading a book and forgot the time." "Well Mary," he
replied, "you can go home now and finish it," and with that he
turned and walked off. End of story? No, not at all because they
both found life miserable without the other, made up and were
happily married within twelve months.

CHAPTER 9
ON THE ROAD COUNTRYWIDE

Gladys and I were very happy in our new life together, although she was on her own all day as I still returned to the warehouse with the morning orders and had my lunch there at midday. In 1939, Jerome McAuliffe was offered a full-time job with Imperial Tobacco (who had taken over Clarke's Tobacco) and I was offered his job. I was both delighted and desolate. Having started in the business "putting up" Jerome's orders I already knew the territory that he covered but that also meant I would only be at home for the weekends. Of course it meant a substantial increase in my salary and commissions and an increase in expenses to run a better car. The area of the No.7 ledger comprised of the Dingle Peninsula (from Castlegregory to Dingle on the north side and Listowel to Annascaul on the south side) for one week.

It included part of North Cork (centred in Boherbue, including Kiskeam, Banteer and a collection of small villages and wayside shops and "all Cathedral cities in between") for the second week. The third week comprised of Rathmore and Knocknagree, Ballydesmond, Gneeveguilla, Castleisland and other villages and wayside shops. The fourth journey started outside Buttevant and was centred in Dromcollogher, taking in Meelin and a wide range of similar character. For the fifth week I went to County Tipperary, starting in Galbally, taking in Emly and on to Tipperary town which was not included in my territory. From there to Donohill, Cappawhite, Doon and Cappamore and up into the hills to Rear Cross, Kilcommon and Hollyford. I had no really large towns and had very tough country roads and poor accommodation to contend with. For the record, my fellow travellers in Musgrave Brothers at that time were: Willie Crawford (No. 1 book), Jim Robinson (No. 2

book), Willie O'Connell (No. 3 book), No. 4 was reserved for inter-wholesaling business for trading with one another if one was out of stock of some item, J. G. Kilpatrick (No. 5 book) and Joe McCullogh (No. 6 book), who besides East Cork also worked Clare and out to Clifden in Co. Galway. My new role as No. 7 completed the cover-age of the South of Ireland.

My new job was also welcome for quite another reason, as Gladys and I were expecting the arrival of our first child. In due course, on 22 June 1939, Jean Gladys was born. As was to be the case with all my children, I was away on a journey at the time of her birth.

Bigger events were soon to overtake, not only Gladys and me, but all of the country and Europe. This was because on the morn-ing of 3 September 1939, England declared war on Germany, who, under Hitler's merciless ambitions had overrun Austria, Czechoslovakia and then Poland. Ireland (under the government of Mr Eamon de Valera) was to declare itself neutral, but there was the ever-present danger that we could be invaded. We all knew that very tough times lay ahead and there would be many shortages of essential commodities. In the meantime I bought a gleaming new green Ford Prefect car and set off with Mr Hugh Musgrave to be introduced to all my new customers. As there was a gap of a few months between Jerome's departure and my appointment, Hugh Musgrave had been covering the territory temporarily. Hugh and I got on very well together and he remained with me for two com-plete journeys totalling ten weeks in all.

This I much appreciated as it was all new to me and very differ-ent in so far as previously I had been selling to most accounts on a weekly basis and now I had to adjust to selling a full five week stock if I could! The range was also entirely different, particularly as Jerome (due to being an agent for tobacco as well) had tended to concentrate on larger items such as cases of matches, tea, sugar, pearl barley and cases of fruit.

Our last week together found us in Castleisland and there was a travelling roadshow in town. As was quite usual in country areas we had to work late and our last call was to Mrs C, who ran one of the best shops in town. Not alone was she a good businesswoman, she had a splendid manner and a tremendous sense of humour.

On the evening of the roadshow we all went for a look around and she and Hugh Musgrave had their fortunes told. Already possessed of quite a large family, she was now expecting again after a gap of several years and to our utter amazement, when we called the following morning and enquired whether there had yet been an arrival her husband replied, "Yes, there are two – Norah presented me with twins this morning." I then asked Hugh about his fortune and he said, "She told me I would soon face some very dangerous situations." She was to be proved accurate because in a few years he was on the high seas in the Royal Navy in the middle of a bitter war.

War strikes

The country representatives earned anything up to £1,000 a year and to get this into perspective it is necessary to compare values then and now. Taking the old currency of pounds, shillings and pence compared with the present decimal currency, the prices were as follows: the Cork Examiner cost 1p then. A dozen eggs then cost 3p. Petrol was 9p a gallon, cigarettes 9p for twenty. So, £1,000 a year worked out to be £35,000 or £40,000 today.

In Ireland, we soon had problems and so had I. Petrol almost disappeared and my Ford was confined to the garage sitting on four blocks of wood. Once again the ever fertile brain of John L. Musgrave came into play. He petitioned the Government to allow some petrol to deliver essential supplies, i.e. tea and matches. Of course, he succeeded. We managed to purchase a few vans and I got a 22 horsepower Bedford Half-Ton that was to prove my lifeline. We had a new addition to our workload now as each Saturday afternoon we loaded our vans with various packages and this took several hours. Working six days a week with only Sunday off was hard on my good wife but she did not complain and often went with Jean to our "free" home in Roches Point as I was now senior staff. In fact we were able to avail of the house for the whole summer as other staff did not care for the place. We loved it. It was while there that Michael Roche informed her that war had been declared by England. Despite the possible air attacks on the nearby forts, she stayed on.

My new job was entirely different and because of petrol scarcity I stayed in many remote villages. Where Hugh and I stayed in Boherbue there was no toilet whatsoever but I changed that soon enough and instead found great accommodation with a Mrs Mulcahy, who was not a customer of Musgraves at all but stuck firmly to our main competitor, Punch & Co. Only for the generosity of my customers I would have starved at times but they were wonderful and on most of my daily journeys provided me with meals. The meals invariably consisted of two boiled eggs and home-made brown bread, and fortunately I enjoyed eggs. On some journeys I brought a Thermos and sandwiches with me on the Monday, but for the rest of the week it was boiled eggs for breakfast, dinner and tea. I nearly came home to Gladys crowing like a rooster! One of my customers got to know of this and would shout to his wife on seeing me arrive, "Here he comes again – two boiled eggs and two boiled eggs and two boiled eggs."

On my Dromcollogher journey, I stayed at the West End Hotel which boasted the only flush toilet in town. I can verify that it also had the hardest bed I have ever slept on. This was rectified with a sprung mattress – but no base board. It took quite some persuading to get them to realise that a base board was a necessary part of the equipment.

The Royal Hotel in Tipperary town provided me with good accommodation on my Tipperary journey and in Cappawhite and Cappamore I stayed in guesthouses. For the Rathmore journey though I was back to customers again.

Dingle was my furthermost outpost and the heaviest with no less than 120 calls. I left Cork at 8.00am and my first call was in Castlegregory – 90 miles further on. I took in every village and shop from there to Cloghane and Brandon, and from there over the mighty Connor Pass to Dingle where I usually arrived at about 8.00pm. I was not finished then either. After my meal I made another call to Hannah O'Dowd next door and then I got my orders together and made out my cash lodgement for the next day.

The Connor Pass was formidable in winter as the narrow road literally clung to the mountain side. It was said that it was constructed by convict labour. Once I had evidence of how it was built as during torrential rain and floods chunks were swept away revealing foundations of flat stones standing upright side by side! Another evening I got a puncture while at the top of the Pass and there was a gale gusting in from the Atlantic. I changed the wheel in five minutes and it took a double brandy to restore my circulation when I arrived at Benner's Hotel.

I usually spent a few days working the town and then headed out west to Brandon, Ballyferriter, Dunquin and around Slea Head to Ventry. All very long days indeed. On Friday morning I cleared up for my trip home. Credit was common and while some cleared in full to benefit of the 3.75 per cent discount, others did not and it was usual to call at the end of the journey to get as big a chunk of money as they could accumulate during the week. I took in Listowel and Annascaul on the way home and had a meal at the commercial travellers' "home from home" – The Glebe in Killarney – and then it was a straight run home over the county bounds.

War Grinds Unrelentlessly On

As the war in Europe intensified, supplies of goods got scarcer and scarcer and many disappeared off the market entirely. Tea and sugar were rationed, coupons were issued to control the sale of clothes and detergents, and the selling of these entered an entirely different stage of sharing out what was available. Tea supplies became a huge problem for many retailers. Their quota was based on the purchases for the year before the war broke out and was not nearly enough to supply all customers with the meagre ration of two ounces per person per week. This was largely due to the restrictions of movement caused by the unavailability of petrol as private cars were practically off the road. This meant that people had to shop locally unless they had a horse and trap or some other means of transport to get them into the nearest town.

John L. Musgrave, with remarkable foresight (I often said he could see around corners), had bought all the tea he could possibly get and there was an excellent stock. I soon found out that the Department of Trade would increase a retailer's quota if he put forward a good case – provided that a supplier was available. Here was a marvellous opportunity for me and I successfully made hundreds of applications for larger tea quotas.

I made agreements with the retailers concerned that they, in return, would give me the bulk of their business. As getting an increased quota earned them many new customers they were delighted and in most cases honoured their word and my order book grew bigger and bigger. Needless to say, other representatives lost out and one in particular took action. In certain areas I began to suffer a lot of pressure from customers who accused me of having supplies of scarce commodities and giving them none. I was puzzled as their allegations were totally untrue; but I soon found out the cause – an opposition representative was resorting to a dirty tricks campaign. He was dropping hints such as saying that he had heard Musgrave had got a big delivery of sultanas and that they should ask for some. I soon shut him up as two can play at that game.

Some extraordinary substitution commodities began to emerge and as the horse and cart had to be used axle grease was essential but unobtainable. But, some genius concocted a substitute that was more like tar than grease and did the job. Also, there was a fake coffee that tasted nothing like coffee but wasn't a bad drink.

One evening in Benner's Hotel, I sat down to my favourite meal of Dingle sole on the bone. Dingle Bay sole has the finest flavour in the world due to the quality of the plankton. Margaret, the waitress, had just placed the delicious looking dish before me and I was about to sprinkle on pepper when my sensitive nose stopped me. I slipped the canister into my pocket and ate my dinner without the pepper. Then I went to find the proprietress Marjorie Benner, a very good friend of mine. On taking out the canister and sprinkling a little on my hand, I asked if it was even a pepper substitute and she replied that she had bought it from me. I enquired where she kept it and she led the way to the storeroom and pointed to a big jar. "My goodness," she said, "it smells very queer". "Indeed," I said, "it doesn't smell queer, it actually is powder for killing cockroaches!". They had got the jars mixed up and she told me that it had been on the dining-room table for months and no one had complained. So much for good taste!

White flour was scarce, but was available on the black market and so white bread was one pound a loaf – an enormous price then as bread was usually eight pence. Bicycles also became scarce and in the town of Castleisland there was a beautiful lady's bicycle on display in a shop window, with no price on it of course. On enquiring, one was told that it could be had for a half chest of tea or a couple of hundredweight of sugar. Very expensive bicycle indeed!

Moving around the country as I did, I had many advantages. I could still get bastible bread as this was made with home milled brown flour. Butter was also scarce, but a creamery friend of mine informed me that butter made from the milk of cows who grazed on early spring grass would keep without refrigeration for six months – and he was right. He gave me a twenty-eight pound box and I put it on a cold floor in the house and it proved it. Some of my customers had stock of now unobtainable items like Wellington boots and horseshoe nails and were quite happy to sell them to me to supply other willing customers.

On one occasion my brother Bill was working in Newcastle West and as I was in Drumcollogher at the same time. We said we would meet. We didn't realise that it was the Fair Day and the hotel was booked out. As we were well known the proprietor said we could use one of the family bedrooms and had his daughter guide us to it. We went to the pictures, had a few drinks, and then decided to turn in for the night. Curiosity killed the cat and we opened the wardrobes to see what they had inside. They were filled with frocks, etc. – and a corset. Nothing else would do now only to try it on, but as I squeezed in to it there was a knock at the door and a female voice asked if she could come in. I dashed into the bed and she came in apologising and went over to the wardrobe.

She was rummaging around and then we realised what she was looking for was at the same time squeezing the life out of me! She left disappointed while we were in convulsions of laughter for hours after. Bill always said he could have enjoyed the evening better if I had not been there!

One day I was working in the village of Liscarroll and stopped my van at the bottom of the hill where the main street ran. As I was about to enter a shop a car started to move at the top of the hill and, as I stood transfixed, it proceeded down across the road and collided with a loud bang with my misfortunate van. I rushed over ready to berate the senseless driver, only to find, to my utter astonishment, that there was none! What happened was that the lady driver had forgotten to put on the handbrake firmly as she parked the car. The radiator was shoved in and I was in real trouble. However, I called John L. and he said, "Stay where you are and I'll send help." A few hours later our company mechanic, Tommy Turpin, arrived with a replacement which he soon fitted and I carried on with my journey just a few hours late. Such a man was John L. Musgrave.

Because of the scarcity of petrol, anyone who had a vehicle got some strange requests. My most extraordinary concerned a very nice family near Castlegregory. Mary and Pat and their four children had a small farm and he also fished while she ran the shop. One morning when I called, instead of the bright cheerful person she was, I found a very sad and disturbed woman. She had been through a terrifying ordeal a few weeks previously. The family had all retired for the night and she said that she did not know what had awoken her, "It must have been the good Lord," she said. For there, looming above her, in the half light, stood her husband with a long knife in his raised hand. She screamed, "Pat, Pat, don't, don't." He seemed to emerge from a trance, dropped the knife, and collapsed crying on the bed. It took some time before he could speak and then he told her that he did not know what had got into him, but his intention was to do away with the family and then himself. I was deeply shocked because a more devoted couple I did not know. Then she told me he had been committed to Killarney Mental Hospital for treatment and further examination.

Some months later I got a telephone call to the business and it was Mary. "I know Mr C that you will be coming our way next week," she said. "I have had good news of Pat, he has been dis-charged and can come home. Would you ever call for him and bring him to us?" I immediately said I would and asked her to inform him to be ready on the following Monday around ten o'clock. I wondered a little apprehensively about what it would be like collecting such a man from a lunatic asylum. I need not have worried, he was delighted to see me. No remarks were made regarding the near tragedy but we talked about everything else all the way to his home. He made a perfect recovery and I continued to do business with them until I left that journey.

Swaps and Innovations

As war progressed, essential items became scarcer and scarcer; to get half a pound of dried fruit at Christmas was like a gift from heaven. Fuel became a daily problem, electricity and gas were only available at certain limited times. Clothes washing presented almost insurmountable problems. Like many, we used a sawdust fire. This consisted of a five gallon metal drum being obtained and this in itself was difficult. The lid was cut off and a one inch hole drilled in the bottom. Into this was inserted a pole and the drum packed tight with damp sawdust, then the pole was removed.

By placing the drum on a few stones and lighting a small fire underneath it, the sawdust would soon burn up the middle hole. The bath of washing was placed on top and in due course, after about an hour, the water began to boil. To get any form of washing powder, coupons were necessary and as the sawdust fire had to be used outside, a fine day was absolutely essential.

Couples planning a wedding often paid others for their clothes coupons in order to obtain a suitable outfit. Petrol became very difficult and expensive on the black market. I often had not enough to get to many outside places. I wrote to customers in advance advising that I'd be at certain crossroads or villages at approximate times and someone would meet me with the orders. Sometimes it would be a female member of the family and this was especially welcome as I would catch up on all the local gossip. I was continually surprised at what happened in these areas, somehow one forgets that we are all much the same – more or less! I was even forced to bring my bicycle with me and cycle around at times. Most travellers only worked towns accessible by the very infrequent and unreliable trains and buses. One of these told me of the longest game of poker he ever took part in and I witnessed the end.

It began at Cork station, interrupted for a while when trains were changed at Mallow for Tralee and continued until they got there. Having reached Dingle by bus and had a meal, play resumed and as I came down for breakfast the following morning, they were just finishing up!

Another friend of mine told me that he was waiting at Buttevant station for a train that he did not expect for several hours and to his surprise one came along and stopped. On getting in he passed a remark, "She is early today isn't she!", only to get the hilarious reply, "It isn't today's train – it's yesterday's!"

One of my worst experiences began one Thursday afternoon in the village of Scartaglen in Kerry when my back tyre got punctured. Fortunately, it carried me to the door of my customer Dan Buckley who was a most helpful chap and immediately lent a hand. We pulled out the spare, but it too was flat; so we stripped off the tyres. The tube on the spare had a lot of petrified punctures and was utterly useless and the punctured tyre had pulled the valve out of the tube. My resourceful friend was not to be defeated and he carefully cut a small hole further along the tube and relocated the valve, putting a neat seal around it. He then put a large patch over the hole where the valve originally was located. As I watched in trepidation, he replaced the tube, pumped it up and we put it onto the car. "Now," he said, "you are all right again, my boy, and good luck to you."

Miraculously, it got me to Killarney and was still fine when I set off for Cork the next morning. Words could not describe my feelings – should I crawl along carefully or go as fast as I could and as far as it would carry me? I was sweating like a horse from sheer anxiety. It was slowly losing pressure and I had to stop and pump it up near Coachford. It carried me to the head of the Straight Road outside Ballincollig when it finally gave up altogether. Locking the van and tucking my briefcase under my arm, I set off on "Shank's Mare".

It was a very warm day and the Lee Fields were full of people out for a swim. I was lucky to meet someone I knew and I asked for a loan of his bicycle. He told me I could take it, but not to be long as he was supposed to be working! I cycled to Victoria Cross and phoned my friends in Lee Garage, then on Merchant's Quay. Within the hour, one of the partners – my good friend Albert Jeffery, arrived with a new tube (God knows where he got it). I finally made home and I can tell you, I slept well that night.

Tragedy Strikes at Home

Other big events were taking place in my home life. My wife's father, John Storey, passed away on the 27 January 1941, and a few months later my mother-in-law came to live with us. Despite our common loss, she was very welcome and great company for my wife. This was especially so in 1942, when on 19 June our second daughter, Marjorie Elizabeth, was born. My mother-in-law was a very considerate woman and ever mindful of other people's needs, a fine character indeed, and a useful addition to our little household. I felt much more at ease as I headed out on a Monday morning.

Unfortunately, we were not to have the pleasure of her presence for too long. On 21 November 1943, I was in Dingle after completing a long and arduous journey around Slea Head and was sitting down to a well earned meal when Peggy, the waitress, said quite casually, "Oh, by the way, there was a call looking for you. Your mother-in-law, I think, dropped dead, I forgot to mention it." I was dumbfounded for a moment and too upset to reproach the girl. I knew I had to get to Cork quickly, especially as our third child was due in December. We were lucky it was not a premature birth, but Gladys bore up remarkably well, demonstrating what a sensible woman she is. Her mother had died of a heart attack in the Income Tax Office. On reflection I am surprised that similar events do not occur more often.

It was a sad time so soon after her father's death and Gladys had no family in Cork. There was joy, however, after a quiet Christmas when on 28 December 1943, we were blessed with a son. We called him after his grandmothers' maiden names – Byron (my mother) and Morton (Gladys' mother).

The war ground relentlessly on and my tyres were no longer usable so I took those from my Ford Prefect. These were too small a gauge and I had to drive very carefully to avoid toppling the van over. Once again, my good friends in the Lee Garage saved the day when another partner, Arthur Good, picked up a fine set of almost new tyres from a crashed car. They lasted me until the war in Europe finally drew to a halt with the surrender of the German forces in North West Germany, Holland and Denmark on 4 May 1945. It took a little longer and the terrible destruction caused by the atomic bomb on Hiroshima on 6 August to force the Japanese to

Roches Point at the Eastern side of the entrance to Cork harbour

The Bouy Yard at Roches Point

Bouy Yard and the Lighthouse in relation to the terrace at Roches Point

The terrace showing the house we used (with the porch) and alongside it the house with the pointed windows which was once a place of worship.

The last of our horse and drays leaving Cornmarket Street, driven by Jack Hickey and Paddy Corcoran, helper (1956) *Photo: Courtesy of late Fred White*

The Loading Bay in the Cornmarket Street Premises and some fine examples of early commercial vehicles (1959)

Part of the warehouse in Cornmarket Street showing the raised offices, affording good observation points (1959)

The 'Grand' opening of P.J. Dawson's Self-Service, the first
independent Self-Service in Cork and possibly in Ireland (early 1960's)

PJ Dawson's shop front, Ballyphehane. It is now a cycle shop

Our former premises at Cornmarket Street, which was originally a retail shop (1966)

The entrance to Cornmarket Street. We moved from here on 6 April 1966 and it is now the home of Guys Company Printing Works

Window display, promoting Musgrave Tea, from one of our earliest members
John Riordan, Rathcormack

The Chairman, Jack Musgrave, addressing the gathering on the occasion of the official
opening of Tramore Road in October 1966. L/R – Mr R.A. Branston, Mr P.D. Hickey,
Mr C.B. Gibson, Mr J.R. Musgrave, Mr Stuart Musgrave Snr, Mr Jack Lynch (then
Minister for Finance), Mr Bob van Schaik (VeGe Europe), Mr Hugh Musgrave,
the Author and Mr Alan Wilkie

Mr Jack Lynch addressing the gathering of the official opening of Musgraves Ltd. Tramore Road warehouse (1966)

Mr Hugh Musgrave addressing the guests at the dinner held in the Metropole Hotel following the official opening of the Tramore Road warehouse. L/R – Mr Hugh Musgrave, Mr Bob van Schaik, Mr Stuart Musgrave Snr, Mr Barry Gibson, Mr Jack Musgrave, Mr Jack Lynch, Mr P.D. Hickey and others (1966)

The Author presenting the winner of the Musgrave Painting Competition with a bicycle.
Watched by Barry Collins at his supermarket in Carrigaline (1970)

The Author (cutting the tape), with Seamus Scally and the proprietor, John Riordan, his wife Pru, and staff of their new Self-Service Supermarket in Fermoy (1973)

The Author with Norma O'Sullivan making a presentation of the proceeds of the Annual
V.G. Dinner Dance to Francis Hegarty of the Wheelchair Association of Ireland (1975)

The presentation to Mr Stuart Musgrave Snr to commemorate seventy years with the company. L/R – Mr A.B. Carswell, Mr John Smith, Mr Pat Hickey, Mr Jack Musgrave, Mr Hugh Musgrave, Mr Hugh Mackeown, Mr Stuart Musgrave, Mr Fred Markham, the Author, Mr Ronnie Smith

Mr Jack Musgrave presenting the silver antique rose bowl to the Author on the occasion of fifty years' service to the company. L/R– Mr Fred Markham, Mr Hugh Mackeown, Mr Jack Musgrave, the Author, Mr Hugh Musgrave, Mr John Smith (March 1977)

Presentation to the Author on his retirement as Chairman of V.G. Services, in Dublin on the 5 July 1977. L/R – Mr John Smith, Mr Jack Burke (Nilands of Galway), Mr Brendan Cassidy and Mr Louis Garvey (Garvey & Sons of Drogheda), the Author, Mr Tim Nolan (Central Office), Mr Dan Griffin (Nilands), Mr Ray Coughlan and Mr Frank Campbell (I.M.D.)

Mr Seamus Scally making the presentation to the Author. Seated L – Mr Noel Hanley, Miss Eileen McCarthy. Standing L/R – Mr Paul O'Neill, Mr John McNamara, Mr John Lonergan, Mr Con Carroll, Mr Terence Murphy, Mr John Pettit, Mr Tom Ryan. Seated R – Mr William Cavanagh, Miss Josephine O'Neill (5 July 1977)

The Author with the silver rose bowl and cruet set presented to him to mark fifty years' service with the company (1977)

The Author addressing the guests at his farewell dinner. L/R – Mr Jack Musgrave, Mrs Gladys Creighton, the Author, Mrs Molly Musgrave, Mr Barry Collins

Presentation made at the Dinner in the Metropole Hotel, Cork, to mark the retirement of Mr A.H. Creighton in July 1977. L/R – Mr John Riordan (Retailer in Fermoy), the Author, Mr Jack Musgrave, Mr Barry Collins (Retailer in Carrigaline), Mrs Gladys Creighton, Mr Dan Griffin (Nilands of Galway), Mr Hugh Mackeown (Managing Director of Musgrave Ltd.)

Super Valu / Centra headquarters and warehouse at Tramore Road, Cork (1993)

surrender on the 14 August 1945.

It would be still another few years before things began to resemble normality. The war years were difficult for everyone, but for me they had a bright side. As I worked in remote areas, where life moved slower and the pressure of living was not so great, we were not as short of essentials as most.

I could get an odd few bags of turf or bog deal (old timber preserved in the bog and very inflammable – great to liven up a fire) and I once got the van filled with turf in grateful return for services done in securing a substantial increase in a customer's tea allocation. I got wellington boots for the family and the odd box of butter and white loaves. I was also earning much more. To compensate for loss of earnings on tea and sweets we were not charged for petrol or the up-keep of the vehicle. Furthermore, I was living more cheaply in outlying areas than if I had to stay in town hotels. Bed & Breakfast only cost seven and sixpence and a very substantial lunch was half a crown (two shillings and six pence).

CHAPTER 10

WE MOVE UP A STEP

Gladys and I felt we could afford a change and began looking at houses. Throughout the war, holidays were spent in the Crosshaven area as it was near to Cork and within reach of a horse and trap or a bike. We even travelled in a two-horse open carriage and I well remember cycling on ahead to get the house open before the family and baggage arrived. We had our eye on a very nice detached house on an eighth of an acre situated in Ardfoyle Avenue on the Blackrock Road, a very respectable area and also near a church and school; so we put a bid on this through our solicitor.

We were on holidays in Fountainstown when I got a wire from him telling me he had closed the deal. Any cash I had, on John Musgrave's advice, had been invested in shares. He was a well recognised expert in the Stock Exchange and was very good with advice to me when I had an end of year bonus. It was onto my bike then and off to Cork to see my solicitor first. The price was £1,600 he told me. This would compare with forty or fifty times that today. So, I would need to raise a mortgage or sell my shares.

My next call was to John L. Musgrave who kindly saw me and listened to my story. "What I would like is your advice, Mr John," I said. "What should I sell?" He looked me straight in the eye, "No need to sell anything, Creighton," he said, "just tell Miss Goodwin to write a cheque for the amount you want and I will sign it and we can see how things turn out at the end of the year." All I could say was, "That is very generous of you and I do appreciate it." He smiled and opened the door for me to pass into his secretary's office. The end of the story is even better, I was never charged one penny interest, such was the great contradiction in John L.'s nature.

He could be as tight as two pence or as magnanimous as a king. We moved house on 17 August 1945, and aptly named it "Journey's End".

It is of interest to note that Mr Stuart Musgrave resided at the entrance of the same avenue. His father (also named Stuart) was one of the founder members of the company along with John L. Musgrave's father Thomas.

The end of the war meant a break for the fighting men, including thousands of American and Canadians who got leave, pending arrangements to ship them home. There was little to entice them to stay in England, so why not see world famed Killarney? And they did – in huge numbers. Every hotel and guesthouse was packed out, there was lots of money to spend and the town's people got rich.

Unfortunately, some of the girls got pregnant and it was a standing town joke that some of next year's crop of babies would have American accents!

During this time I witnessed racial prejudice. Some service men were black and as such were completely socially ostracised. This I found hard to understand as in my book colour or creed did not matter.

The availability of goods slowly improved and with it, competition for trade increased. My customers did not forget my concern for their problems during the Emergency and I began to develop a very good connection. Petrol supplies also increased, but in 1947 I still struggled to get about in my Bedford van – now in great need of a re-bore and also new steering – as the ball ends were only held together with rubber bands. I carried dozens of spare spark-plugs and when the engine oiled up I fitted a new set and carried on as far as these would go. Winter 1947 saw the biggest snow fall I ever had to contend with. It snowed from mid-January right through to March and I had a terrible time as my journeys were in out-of-the-way places and on little used roads.

Just at the beginning of the terrible weather, Hugh Musgrave

returned from service in the Royal Navy and was anxious to famil-
iarise himself with the business. He had arranged to spend a week
or so "on the road" with me. We set off on the Rathmore journey
and succeeded in getting as far as Killarney by Tuesday, having
started outside Millstreet and covered Rathmore and some outlying
places in between.

On Wednesday we set out for Castleisland and it snowed all day,
so it was with great difficulty that we got to Scartaglen and back to
Killarney for the night. Thursday we made it back to Rathmore, to
find the road to Knocknagree blocked by a wall of snow. In antici-
pation, we had brought our wellington boots and, as it was only
five miles, I suggested that we should walk there and we did. Hugh
was nothing if not game and it was quite an experience plodding
up the hill as the day was fine but the snow was up to eight or ten
inches in places. The people in Knocknagree were surprised to see
us as they were isolated. The road out of the village to
Ballydesmond was blocked by a huge snow drift in the middle of
which was someone's car.

Having done our business, we found that the village was out of
bread and the men were organising a small truck and some shovels
to try and reach Rathmore, so we agreed to help them. After some
skidding and a bit of shovelling we eventually got there. Next
morning I suggested a long, but possible, detour to get to
Ballydesmond to complete our journey. Hugh gave me one hard
look and real navy fashion said, "Creighton, you just get me back to
Cork. Now, that is an order." He told his Uncle, John L., that he
would never go out with me again and he didn't!

I became an expert at getting out of skids, but could not have
carried on were it not for John L. who gave me his own set of snow
chains. No one but he would have had such a thing in Southern
Ireland, where snowy winters only occur every five or six years.

Returning to More Normal Times
Shortly after the thaw set in I met my predecessor, Jerome McAuliffe,

in Kanturk one evening. Our journeys crossed frequently; he was a great friend and put in many a good word for me with our customers.

This particular evening we went for a walk and had a few drinks before retiring. Next day I had a horrible problem with my driving and found myself drifting to the wrong side of the road. I was not drunk, nor had we over-indulged the previous evening and it was very frightening. I was glad to make it to Cork and the company mechanic without an accident, but only because there was little traffic. Tommy Turpin said he would investigate and I went to the office. To my surprise on my return, he told me he could find no fault in the steering. We went for a run and, of course, the trouble was still there. He then decided to jack up the car altogether off the ground and on doing so he discovered the real trouble. The rear axle had a play of half an inch or so in it. Evidently the pull and drag of the snow chains had caused this and the U-bolts had shifted so, in fact, the van was steering itself from behind.

I was delighted as cars became available and I purchased a new Hillman – a car with a great reputation – and so did my friend Jerome. The next time we met I asked him how he liked the car. "That's not a car it's a thing," he said, "and it has me driven mad. Without warning the steering wheel jumps about and I have to stop. It keeps on happening." Apparently the workers making the vehicles had little or no engineering experience, as most of the trained workers lost their lives in the war. So, we had to get rid of our Hillmans; he got a Ford and I got a reliable Austin.

Tea was available again and the fight for trade resumed. Our tea blender, Alan Wilkie, an Englishman trained in London, and I became closely associated. I carried a good selection of different priced blends in square tin boxes and many customers had exclusive blends specially mixed to suit the water in their district! There was a lot of mumbo-jumbo about tea and we all claimed to be experts.

My friend Jerome had a method of helping me get a large share of sales. He was a big boned fellow and on seeing a tea chest outside a shop counter, as was common, he would give it a mighty kick and if it was empty he said, "I hope you gave Creighton the order." As cigarettes and tobacco were still on quota, Jerome had a few aces to play and they knew it – so I got my share of the orders.

Jerome was quite a character and often said that the best way to know when you needed a new suit was when the pockets of the old one would hold no more notebooks. Similarly when he changed cars he got new samples of everything and simply left the old samples in the old car. A garage owner in Newmarket confirmed this saying he got enough smokes for three months when he supplied Jerome with a new car.

Jerome and I had a sort of a secret joke and when we would meet he would say, "Aren't you gone home yet?" and we would both roar with laughter. This related to an actual experience he had while staying in Breens in Knocknagree. He was going through the bar on his way out at around 10.00am and he passed a solitary figure at the bar with a pint in front of him. Jerome knew the man and bid him "good morning" but got no reply. On returning to lunch the man was still there but again gave no reply to Jerome's greeting. The same happened when he returned at about 8.00pm. When going to bed he again passed through the bar and the man was still there. "Aren't you gone home yet?" asked Jerome to get the withering reply, "It's equal and shit to you".

Tom MacBrateney had died suddenly and had been replaced by his son Bill, a very different character. He had an excellent brain and was a good buyer without any of the sarcasm of his illustrious father. He and I got on great. Should he be in doubt about the saleability of an item he would consult me; if I said it would sell he would buy and I made it my business to sell it. Neither of us made many mistakes and from him I got all the market news and knew in advance of probable price increases. This was a very valuable selling point. I now knew my customers very well and each was a different character and required different treatment. Each area also had different needs. In remote areas, the commercial traveller was often the only contact outside their own community and doing business relied greatly on whether they liked him or not.

I had long realised that a good manner was essential and that a smile or a good laugh could work wonders. A stock of stories and the knack of telling them was an asset, but one had to be very careful as to the type of story. Some would not appreciate a double meaning or sex related yarn, while others looked forward to hearing nothing else. With others, definitely no stories, just business.

The commercial traveller was king in his own territory and the business of the company depended on his skills. Should I find items selling that we did not carry, Bill would obtain them and I would sell them. One example was in an area entirely outside grocery. I knew that there was a huge trade in washing soda and blue stone – the two ingredients for making spray to prevent blight on the potato crop at that time. Bill and I decided to go after it. Very soon I had wagons of each delivered to centrally located railway stations, with instructions for the station master to deliver in varying quantities to our customers. It was a useful business to develop in the spring as from January to May money was tight.

My knowledge of the hardware trade was also very valuable and I soon started selling steel buckets for milk, churn and yard brushes and even animal medicines. Grocery was quiet after Christmas and this extension of the business was very valuable.

The Night After the Races

Another of our travellers, Fred Rohu, had the town of Killarney in his journeys and he and I often met there. Fred was a great character and we had much in common to discuss, being in the same business, and we looked forward to meeting. It was a peculiarity of the business that, for perhaps a year, you would meet the same representative and then Christmas would change the rota and a whole new bunch would emerge. You might not meet your earlier friends for several years.

Killarney races were always a problem and one was lucky to get a bed. The Glebe Hotel, where we all stayed, had an annex and on one race week I was located there. The rooms ran off a central corridor and at the end was a toilet. The town was no place to be on such occasions and so I went to bed early. I was awakened by a loud voice with an English accent yelling, "£2,000 old boy, not a penny less". This went on so long I could not stand it, so I got up and opened the door to see the owner of the voice. He was standing on the toilet seat leaning out of the window bargaining over the price of a car in the yard below. I gave him a nudge and on gaining his attention said, "You know, I am trying to get some sleep up here". He jumped down and said, "Awfully sorry, old chap, I will go below now, but it will cost the bugger £500 more!"

Tough Times

While John L. Musgrave had many good points, he had little regard for the human side of his travellers' lives. The working week then covered five and a half days – the half day being Wednesday. John kept very careful scrutiny of all accounts and saw his representatives on Saturday afternoon. This meant Sunday was the only day that I, or any of the others, had free.

John first saw each traveller privately when the week's trade was discussed. Every six months we got a card showing our weekly turnover and profit for that period in the previous year. Each week we got a slip of paper showing the previous week's sales compared with the previous year's, the aggregate figure and the current situation to date plus or minus. We got our tea sales and factory sales and there was usually a short discussion on how you stood.

John wouldn't listen to any difficulties or excuses. Once on telling how tough the competition was, I got the answer, "Scratch a little deeper Creighton". Then you went into the main office where, with the office manager, Jimmy Crowley, and the credit controller, Christy Newman, your ledger was carefully perused for any accounts that were slipping into too much credit. Each representative was held responsible if he allowed this to happen. There was a problem as customers usually gave an order first and then paid some amount off the account. In borderline cases if the order exceeded the cash, thus increasing the amount left outstanding, the order would be arbitrarily reduced by Christy Newman or Jimmy Crowley. This led to heated disagreement. John L. just stood and said nothing until the recriminations ceased but the whole open plan office was eagerly listening. It wasn't an encouraging atmosphere, especially if it was a bad year for the farming community, on whom we largely depended.

Credit was how business was done. Our customers had to give credit and during the winter months those in the dairy industry had no milk to sell and not much money coming in, the shopkeeper had to wait – and so had we. Many of the larger farmers settled accounts once a year, indeed, John L. himself only settled his household accounts once a year! The supplier, at least, was sure of that money!

The war had affected almost every family, so the Creighton family were no exception. My sister had lost her husband, a prisoner of war on the Japanese prison ship *Lisbon Maru*, and she and her two boys were evacuated from Hong Kong to Manila and then to Australia. Reception facilities were poor. They had a hard and worrying time and she had to get a job to supplement the meagre army allowance. In 1948, they returned to Dublin but unfortunately, all the suffering had taken its toll as she was in ill health and died in September 1949.

The burden of taking care of her two boys, Jeffrey, then 18 and Ronnie 15, fell on my shoulders as the other executor of her will administrator was my elder brother, Charles. The elder boy was in the final stages of qualifying as a motor mechanic and remained in Dublin. I fought with the British Ministry of Pensions and succeeded in obtaining sufficient funds to educate Ronnie in Mountjoy School in Dublin and he spent his holidays with us. The boys were used to their own ways due to living in the Far East and having servants to meet their beck and call. However, Ronnie was a good worker and did well at school. He failed to get into the Airforce as they discovered he was colour blind, but I got him to do a bursary examination for Trinity College, he succeeded and went on to obtain an engineering degree.

Book 3
The Final Challenge

CHAPTER 11

I MEET TROUBLE

Business was thriving for me, but I was working very long hours. The method of getting as big an order as possible meant literally taking stock mentally and going over a book, listing our full range and, as the customer had to attend to his customers at the same time, this extended the process. A good order could take over an hour to obtain. In these circumstances it was often better for both customer and traveller to do business when the shop was shut. This meant a twelve hour day and, with only Sunday left to yourself, it was a terrible strain.

All the additional worries and pressures after my sister's death were too much for me and one day I was travelling along a country road towards a place called Gullane Cross near Rathmore, Co. Kerry, when I was taken ill and only just made it to a customer's door. They kindly made me a cup of tea and gave me some aspirin and I decided to try and get to Rathmore. It was about eight o'clock and getting dark, being March, and the wife said to her husband, "Dan, wouldn't you go with him?". "Indeed I won't woman," he replied, "he might go over the ditch, do you want me to get killed?"

Nevertheless, I made it to Mrs Linehan who ran the Post Office in Rathmore and also provided accommodation for a few travellers. She fetched a doctor who gave me some sedation and advised me to try and get to Cork for a thorough examination. I was fortunate the next day as two locals had some business in Cork and drove me home. I was in the middle of a serious nervous breakdown.

It was 1951 and I was not yet 40 years old, but almost overnight I became like an old man. I lost confidence in my ability to walk and tottered along with the aid of a walking stick. I lost my appetite and found it difficult to sleep and were it not for the realisation that

I had a wife and family to think of, I might have lost my reason as well.

There was little that the medical profession had to offer then. There was a wide range of "remedies", mostly sedatives, to try and calm the system down but the difficulty was to try and find one that didn't have any bad side effects.

My doctor was a very open-minded man and told me that the cure lay mostly with myself. I had to take myself in hand, get my mind fixed on positive things and develop the will to get back to normal. Privately, he told Gladys not to give me too much sympathy, as I felt very sorry for myself and as such this was good advice. Sympathy would only have helped to confirm my own dreadful fears.

Encouragement and understanding was what I got and after four months of hell I finally decided that the best cure was work. Unable to drive, the company provided a driver for me and I began the slow and difficult path to recovery. It was up and down as I was never great in the mornings, I improved a little as I got down to doing business and took my mind off myself, but the nights were very difficult. I can remember once in Dingle hearing the town clocks strike every hour during the night, but I still managed to carry on with the job.

One of my drivers was John Trinder whose brother Jim also worked for the company. Solid, reliable lads they were, but brought up in a very strict household where children were only allowed speak when spoken to. I experienced this on one of my journeys to Dingle. I thought that I would find out how long it would take for him to speak to me. Apart from "Good morning, Mr Creighton," there was not a word spoken from Cork to Tralee! That must be a record. Another of my drivers was Paddy Simpson who had just joined the company and was delighted to get away from the monotony of compiling orders.

There was plenty of conversation with Paddy who was a very nice chap and we got on great. He was blessed with a splendid manner and as such destined for "the road", beginning travelling in the city and in time getting a full country journey.

It took twelve months before I was fully recovered and as my doctor had predicted, I emerged a better person. I had a much better understanding of other people and became a listener as well as a talker, more conscious of other people's problems and altogether a more mature personality.

I Lose My Dad, My Best Friend

For quite some time now we now had had had four Mr Musgraves in the company. John Laird was still Head of Affairs, his cousin Stuart (Hugh's father) was Secretary, Hugh was in the business, and now we also had John's son – John Roberts Musgrave – known as Mr Jack. By combined action we succeeded in getting John to change his routine and at long last we were able to finish at around one o'clock on Saturdays.

My father, who had watched my career with great interest, had by now retired. There was no pension scheme then and John, whose own health was failing, had made no provision for people retiring. To their everlasting credit, Stuart Musgrave and Jack continued to pay my father a salary until his death on 27 December 1951. It had been a difficult and sad year, but he left us with wonderful memories. A kind and considerate man, so generous he often left himself short, a man of high principles and reflecting his love of the game as a Cork County cricketer, his motto was, "Always play a straight bat". We missed him greatly.

I Lose Another

After my nervous breakdown I never brought home the business on weekends. Weekends were for gardening, taking Gladys for a night out and a little rest. One Saturday afternoon, on 1 March 1959, I got delivery of a trailer of farmyard manure from a farmer friend and was busy helping the gardener to tidy it up into a heap when a telegram arrived. The sad news was that my father's brother Arthur (after whom I was named) had passed away.

He had never married and had been an English teacher to naval cadets on a training ship anchored in the Mersey River near Liverpool. The *H.M.S. Conway* was an old sailing man-of-war. He had been retired for a number of years and lived in Abergeley in North Wales, and he and I corresponded regularly. A fine character and well educated, he loved his work and a game of golf. I was the only relative at the funeral and the cremation, and I thought it a most moving experience. The coffin rested where an altar would normally have been situated in the little chapel and as the service proceeded it was moving, almost imperceptibly until soon it was no longer there. His gold Waltham hunter watch and chain are now family heirlooms.

Jack Musgrave was by now starting to take over the running of the business and it was to him that we now reported. He was quite different from his father and had a better knowledge of everyday affairs and a much more reasonable attitude to people's problems. By know I produced not alone the largest turnover but, also, the biggest profits, as my years of constant endeavour were now paying off. Within a few years, in 1955, John Laird Musgrave had passed away and Jack was in full command.

My father had always said that I was "Johnny's white-haired boy" – perhaps I was, but I was also his Number One traveller. He sometimes spoke of his own days on "the road" in the days of trains and jaunting cars. When he was developing the business he spent Monday to Friday travelling, Saturday ordering and Sunday doing his books. He had a great affection for Dingle as he originally opened up the territory and it was one of our best journeys.

He told me how he had once overcome a near collapse of our sales in the area. Apparently there was a local feud between some families in the town and it was a bitter affair. Unfortunately, John was known to be very friendly with one family that was "blacked". The town people decided to "black" him too and to stop trading with him. A friendly customer told him about this, so what would he do? His plan was absolutely brilliant. He sat down on the Sunday and wrote out five or six fictitious orders in his order book. Reaching Dingle, his first customer paid her account and said, "You know you won't be getting any orders in town Mr Musgrave". "Why ever not?" he asked, "I have already got four or five, here, look at my order book," opening it and placing it on the counter top. "Well, if that is the case what am I fussing about? I never liked the idea anyway," she replied. John was home and dry.

John had some unusual indulgences and if you were a good boy you got a present of some of these. He gave me a small, white, linen pillow to place on top of a usual one – "If you can't sleep you just turn it over. It is cool and you will soon nod off". I also got a woollen half-rug to keep my legs warm in the car as there was no heating system then. I got a bedside table that you could slide over the bed and that had a top that you could be raised and adjusted to hold a book so that you didn't have to hold your arms outside the covers and get cold – no central heating then either! I have both these items in use today.

John also had a good sense of humour. Once I happened to be in the office when a woman customer, who owed us quite a bit, called to see him and I was called in. He had the ledger out on the desk and was telling her in no uncertain terms that it would not do and she would have to find money from somewhere. She was telling a hardluck story ending with "….and to cap my troubles Mr John, I just had my seventh child". "Well woman," he said, "I had nothing to do with that." I couldn't control my giggling and was told instantly there was nothing to laugh about. When she had departed he called me back into the office and roaring laughing he said that he had not reckoned the implications of what he had said!

John Laird Musgrave had a profound influence on my business life, his example, his expertise, his tight control and generosity at times left an indelible mark.

Nearer Home, Much Nicer

My journeys were changed in 1956. I passed Dingle on to Fred Rohu and Tipperary went to another representative. Instead, I now had the Bandon area and one week free to develop a new area starting with Dungarvan and taking in Carrick-on-Suir and Clonmel.

I was delighted to get a home run as I could then go home every night – even if very late. At last I saw more of my family or one of them at least. Jean was now seventeen and boarding at Alexandra College in Dublin. Byron was boarding at Mountjoy in Dublin and Marjorie was the only one still at home, as she was a day pupil at Rochelle School. They were all growing up fast. We now had our own seaside home in our favourite place, Roches Point. We had bought what had been the gatekeeper's lodge above White Bay.

For some time we had felt that we could afford to move from "Journey's End" and acquire a home more in the country. Gladys kept an eye on the "Houses for Sale" advertisements. We looked at quite a few and came across a lovely old house on ten acres (three were gardens) in a place called Kilcully, five miles from Blackpool, on the north side of Cork City. The house was called "Mill House" and the old mill stream ran through the gardens; one original mill still stood in fine condition, a second ruined mill was in the valley below the house and a third lay further down the valley.

In its heyday two of the mills had ground grain and the water had provided power by running straight on the mill wheel on the upper mill and half way on the wheel on the second. By the time it reached the third it only pushed against the bottom of the wheel and produced a much slower type of power and this was ideal for threshing flax. All a part of old Cork! It was a lovely old place and we immediately fell in love with it and bought it in June 1958. We were moving up in the world.

Chapter 12

PROMOTION

Jack Musgrave and I got on extremely well. He began to take me into his confidence and I learned, to my surprise, that overall Musgraves was not doing as well as we would have liked. Towards the end, in 1958, he appointed me General Manager – my travelling days were now over. I had a new and formidable challenge ahead.

Our main competitors were Punch & Company, Newsom & Company, Dwyer & Company, M.D. Daly and Ogilvie & Moore, more or less in that order. An organisation called the Retail Grocers, Drapers and Allied Trades Association – RGDATA, had started up its own distribution business as a co-operative under the name of Merchant's National Co-operative. Their prices were very keen and they began attracting a lot of our customers away from us. We were still using the old "cost intensive" system, as when I first joined the company in 1927, and we gave credit up to three months. We had some two thousand customers but, as was usual for retailers, each company's traveller got a "turn" and orders tended to be small. We had eight men on the road and this meant that prices tended to be higher. Our mark-up was a minimum of 16 per cent and even at that we were not making money.

Jack Musgrave and I set off for England as we had learned that similar problems existed there and we wanted to find out if the English wholesalers had any answers. In Brighton we met a man called Dick Branston, who had introduced a new method of trading called "Voluntary Group Trading" for his employers, Stewart & Company, in 1956. We found him to be very co-operative and he outlined the system to us.

The system was very successful in Europe, but had originated in the USA as far back as 1921 when a Smith Flickinger of

F. M. Flickinger Wholesale Company, Buffalo, New York, had devised the plan. By 1926 Flickingers Red and White stores had gained national popularity. Other organisations followed suit. World War II slowed the growth somewhat, but by 1956 the system had spread to Europe (Belgium, France, Germany, Switzerland and The Netherlands). There started the VeGe Organisation of Mr F. Harin, Mr A. Lamboles, Mr E. Sipkes and Mr L. K. van Schaik. It was with them that Stewart & Company were in close co-operation using the symbol "VG" – simply meaning Voluntary Group.

The concept was born out of adversity, as the multiple chain stores were threatening the very existence of independent retailers and Mr Flickinger rightly perceived that the answer was for retailers and wholesalers to work as one unit. Retailers bought all items carried by the wholesalers from them alone and it provided greater purchasing power, better terms and lower prices – enabling the wholesaler to offer lower prices to the retailer and he, in turn, to his customers, thus competing much more effectively with the multiples.

The wholesaler could also keep retailers up to date on price changes, market conditions and new items and could also organise special promotions. Window bills were placed for regular special offers and hand bills posted in house to house distribution. Whilst there were no self-service shops in Ireland then, we knew that that was not too far away and the wholesalers could lead the way by pro- viding store engineering and development services, site locations and acquisition departments. Financial assistance was also an area in which the wholesaler could help. Advertising and training were all there to be developed.

All this and more was outlined to us by Dick Branston and I was fascinated. Here, surely, was the way forward – I could see it in my mind's eye as a straight road ahead, but, as I rightly conceived, it was uphill. There was a great goal to strive for. Jack and I discussed this privately at length, I told him my thoughts and, like the leader that he was, he straight away said, "Right Arthur, we will do it" – the green light was on.

A Journey of a Thousand Miles
Begins with the First Step

There was much to be done. We had to get our prices down, arrange special offers and support them with hand bills to be distributed door to door and organise a weekly bulletin (this contained not alone weekly offers but instructions for window displays, articles urging retailers to put in new shop fronts, improve the interiors and keep clean and tidy). We also had to introduce the doctrine of lower prices, which meant getting cash in seven days. Remember all this was against a background of where wholesaler and retailer gave credit and window bills or priced goods on display were unheard of. Shops were all still counter-service and many were far from being clean, let alone tidy.

My good friend Bill MacBrateney was invaluable and did trojan work in producing our new price list and arranging the special offers. Compared with today's range of offers these were very simple. Here are a few examples from the 18th – 30th April 1960:

Bird's Custard Tins	@ 1 shilling six pence
Strawberries in tins	@ 2 shillings
Bird's Jellies	@ 9 pence

The following fortnight it was:

Lavender Floor Polish	reduced from 1 shilling, six pence to 1 shilling and three pence
Windowleen	@ 11 pence
Silicone wax	reduced from 1 shilling, six pence to 1 shilling and three pence

And then:

Brasso	@ 9 pence
Carrots	@ 1 shilling and three pence
Irish Stew (Dennys)	@ 2 shillings
Garden Peas	@ 10 pence
Cream Crackers	@ one shilling and three pence

This was all in the old pounds, shillings and pence currency and each offer was accompanied by window bills and hand bills. As the year went on we also introduced new lines in our offers and had double offers such as tinned fruit priced singly at two shillings a tin, or three tins for five shillings and six pence. By August, still using only three items, we began to introduce a list of other bargains for which there was no window bills but for which show cards for shelf use were provided.

The travellers had to be indoctrinated with the new "religion" and so had the retailers. Once more I became a traveller and called on promising retailers, especially those that had good businesses but were customers of the opposition wholesalers. Now I was selling a new system rather than goods. I had good success but it was hard and intensive work and often the retailers were not really listening. The most amusing example of this was in a shop in the Turner's Cross area of the city run by two sisters well known for being tough negotiators and with a substantial business. I was lucky to pick a quiet time and I thought I had the attention of both women as they leant across the counter from me. They let me have my say without interruption for about ten or fifteen minutes and then one turned to the other and said, "You know Julie, if he turned his collar around he would make a neat little priest!" – so much for Voluntary Group Trading.

We held our first meeting of retailers in the Metropole Hotel in May 1960, with Jack Musgrave acting as Chairman. It was well attended and there was a lot of interest.

The following meeting was held on 27 September and some of the points I made are revealing. "We have witnessed a rapid development in this city in the field of modern retailing, the entry of Dunnes Stores into the field of green fruit and groceries, followed by Woolworths in all of their 22 shops nationwide." I had been telling retailers that something like this would happen and although it was in neither of our best interests it did help to speed up the modernisation of our stores.

I also organised country meetings with great care. I would pick an area and our representative would produce a list of all of the better retailers. These, in turn, would be invited to a meeting at a convenient venue. Our representative would arrange transport where necessary and I would address the meeting and answer questions. I quickly learnt that there was still some scepticism and to overcome this I thought of the idea of bringing along three or four already converted retailers who were enthusiastic and were achieving substantial success and much increased turnover in their own stores. This was a good move as retailers had more confidence in what other retailers told them than if it had come from me.

We started our first week in Voluntary Group Trading with two retailers but by September 1960, we had close on 150. We encouraged intending members to visit those already in the movement and this was a great help. We encouraged the use of hand bills by offering 50 free with 200 purchased and we had a levy of ten shillings per member per week to cover window bills.

Self-service came in 1961 when Pat Dawson of St Mary's Stores in Connelly's Road, Ballyphehane, converted. He was followed closely by Pat O'Shea in Cobh. I believe that these were the first two independent self-service shops in Ireland, although today, neither of these two gentleman are in the grocery business. However, both developed excellent businesses in other areas. Before leaving retailing, Pat O'Shea had developed a fine supermarket, now trading under the SuperValu banner in Cobh and run by Eamon Mescella. The effect of this wind of change blowing over a hitherto rather sleepy wholesale and retail scene was dynamic. Whatever else we did, we certainly encouraged a sense of urgency and fervour and it was quite remarkable the pioneering zeal evinced by our retailing friends.

A Sad Event and A Well-Earned Holiday

My brother, Bill, had changed companies and since 1948 was a representative for Musgrave Sweets, the factory being under Mr Hugh

Musgrave, Secretary of the company since 1955. He had taken over the management from his father, Stewart. Bill was very pleased with his new job but in a few years he suffered a traumatic bereavement with the sudden death of his wife, Georgina, on 28 March 1960. We were all deeply shocked as she was very outgoing and full of life. The tragedy was made worse as it occurred in the middle of a game of cards with friends when she excused herself hurriedly and did not return. She had collapsed and died in the bathroom. After this sad event, Bill came to live with us at Mill House for a few years until he was offered a position in Dublin with the jointly-owned tea company, Musgrave Brooke Bond. He accepted, as Cork had only sad memories for him.

The following year we went on holidays to San Remo, Italy, our first without the family and the first outside Ireland for a long time. Marjorie had joined her sister Jean at Alexandra College and this left us free to have a really fantastic time. We stayed in a magnificent villa overlooking the bay, marble stairs, chandeliers and gold fittings in the bathroom – in fact it was the former seaside villa of a relation of the late Tzar of Russia.

We met the Count, a charming man, who occupied the upper floor, and Madam Giovanni who ran the establishment. She had recently been reconciled with her travel agent and was anxious to impress us, her first "English" for a while. Each morning she would ask what we would like for dinner and invite us to discuss dishes from her cookery books. Gladys was introduced to Italian cuisine and I to Italian wines – it was certainly VIP treatment. She was a splendid cook and ran the small hotel with the aid of a man as portly as herself whom she called the Butler but as we found out shared the same room with him as well! The last night we were there we forgot our key and in response to throwing gravel at the windows they both stuck their heads out of the one room.

Returning to Dublin, we stayed overnight with Gladys's brother, Jack Storey, and his wife Jeannie at Masonic Boy's School where he was Headmaster. They were in very good form, preparing to depart to their summer cottage in Delgany and little did we think of impending tragedy as we set off for Cork the following Monday. Jack went to the cottage by himself where he suffered a massive heart attack and by the following Thursday he had failed to respond to treatment and we had a second family loss, at only 52 years of age.

Jack Storey was a brilliant man who had won every bursary and scholarship available at Trinity College, emerging with a Ph.D and fluency in four languages. I had never met anyone with such a prodigious memory. When making arrangements for my sister's burial he had really impressed me. I would enquire about a suitable solicitor or undertaker – whatever – and he would stay silent for a moment or two and then say, for example, "I think Mr X would be best, I met him at a dinner a few years ago and his telephone number was ————, try him". All with no apparent effort. Incidentally, all the Storey family have excellent memories including Gladys. She amazes me with what she can recall.

On returning to Cork, Gladys had occasion to meet her own medical doctor, Dr W. B. Welply. Hearing of the sad events he asked how her blood pressure was. As she did not know he proceeded to check and probably saved her life, for it was above normal and needed remedial action.

Fast Action Breeds Success

Business continued at a hectic pace. The bigger orders were coming along, but costs had to be cut if profits were to result. Hand in hand with retail activity, methods of warehousing, order compilation and delivery had to change. Space became paramount, resulting in the introduction of high rise racking, pallet trucks and our first forklift truck. The man chosen to operate this highly sophisticated (to us at that time) piece of machinery was John Carroll, who became an expert and won the Munster Championships several times and the Lancing Bagnel Trophy. He won third place in all Ireland in the Mobex Exhibition in Dublin ten years later.

Up until this we had the old high cost system so this had to change also. Checking of orders was discontinued and Bridie Taylor, whose job it was and whose motto was "no mistakes", had to be relocated. She proved invaluable in controlling the payment of suppliers, seeing we missed no discounts, and taking the longest credit obtainable. To her day of retirement she still made no mistakes! Of course she was good as she and I were both "finished off" in Coburns Business Academy in Cork.

A printing machine was introduced by Frank Walley and operated by George Devlin. The true cost of deliveries was examined in depth, minimum orders were fixed and deliveries to out-of-the-way places were discontinued – not without some traumatic appeals, but unfortunately there is no revolution without upset. Our first tail-lift was fitted to the latest truck, all of eight tonnes and a monster then. She was a Leyland Beaver, registration number IPO 950, the "Yellow Monster" according to her driver, Mick Hayes.

Many customers collected their own goods and we encouraged this by allowing a discount for carriage. This encouraged callers but upset the warehouse, clogged up the delivery bay with vehicles and necessitated immediate compilation. The modern answer was the Cash & Carry system and we introduced the first in Ireland at our premises in Cornmarket Street in 1961. Well known now, but then it was revolutionary: Collect your own order – pay cash (What?) – Oh, but what low, low prices! It was a roaring success. So, Ireland's first voluntary group emerged, Ireland's first independent self-service retailers and Ireland's first Cash & Carry. We were a company of firsts and were determined to stay that way.

Manufacturers were now beginning to realise that a big change was underway and the more enlightened began to produce smaller packs. They were also being forced to recognise other changes when we began to look for better discounts in return for bigger volume at year end (this is now known as the LTA – long term agreement). For the record, I negotiated our first with Matterson of Limerick, since absorbed by Erin Foods (in 1961). So, within a year or so of introducing VG trading, we were rapidly putting our business into a more efficient shape and gearing up for the supermarket revolution which we spearheaded in the independent sector.

The larger corporate sector was hardly involved in food retailing at all. Across the road in Patrick's Street, Roches Stores kept an eye on their former employee, Ben Dunne. In 1962 they followed him into food retailing. Until then the only large retailers were Liptons, Home & Colonial, Smiths Stores and Woodford Bourne. Later, we were to see 5 Star (D.D. Williams, Tullamore), now absorbed by a still later arrival – Quinnsworth. The battle for the housewife's purse was on.

Consolidation

We obtained the VG franchise from VG Grocery Service, England on 13 June 1962 and it was for the whole of the Republic. The price was mutually agreed at one pound note, now framed and carefully preserved. We were aware of our own limitations and the great potential for bigger buying power if the system was nationwide. In the largest market, Dublin, buying from manufacturers was so easy and encouraged, as most manufacturers were situated there, that the largest wholesaler Shirley Spencer & Belfort had long since ceased trading. Another, Hugh Moore & Alexanders had shrunk to a few agencies. However, we did find a smaller but very sound company called Carton Brothers who were operating out of Dublin and, following discussions with them, then introduced the VG system in 1962.

Regular fortnightly offers were now standard practice, but still limited to three or four lines as it was some time before we could get either manufacturers or retailers to agree more. Discussions and negotiations with manufacturers became day- to-day business. Quantity terms were geared to suit the large retailer rather than wholesaler, even though the latter's purchases were infinitely greater and involved a lower delivery cost.

Furthermore, manufacturers delivered to branch outlets at best prices regardless of the size of the order. All this had to be changed and Willie MacBrateney, Desmond Leavy of Carton Brothers and I spent countless hours in the crusade. I was torn between the two objectives – the battle with the manufacturer and the development of our retailers. The only person who had any retail experience in Musgrave was Fred White, an assistant to Mr Walter Blackwood who ran our retail business. Fred did tremendous work getting new members but he had no experience of self-service.

I kept in very close touch with Dick Branston and his expanding operation in England. I was invited to attend their central office meeting of wholesalers, now numbering five. This was an invaluable experience and I cannot speak too highly of the outstanding support, encouragement and friendliness extended to me. I also met Dr Bob van Schiak, the Director General of VeGe Europe, at some of these meetings. I knew we had to find someone who understood self-service, how to lay out a store, construct and extend stores and who could talk "retail" language.

I mentioned my problem to Bob – a big expansive experienced man who could converse in five languages – he thought and said, "I met a young man at a meeting in Amsterdam who works for RGDA-TA, his name is Pat Hickey. I think you should get in touch with him."

Back in Cork I got busy and had soon made contact with Pat and arranged a very "hush, hush" meeting in the Metropole Hotel in Cork. The arrangement was that he and I and Jack Musgrave would go to a particular room individually at different times. I immediately liked this man. He was frank, to the point and business-like. We talked at great length about his work – travelling the length and breadth of Ireland, converting RGDATA members to self-service. He had won an OEEC (now OECD) scholarship (the only one allocated to Ireland) to study retail and wholesale distribution in America and Europe. He knew how their supermarkets were developed and controlled. We told him what we were about, our plans and ambitions. The one thing that struck me was how, in the present job, he was kept so busy that he seldom, if ever, got to see the final result of his efforts – he had no job satisfaction. I felt that this point was paramount, coupled with what he had seen of VeGe in Holland, in securing his agreement to join us – which he did, in October 1963.

Now I had a man who knew the business and he and I began an outstanding working relationship. Pat Hickey was a tower of strength, a dynamic, magnetic personality and our retailers embraced his sound advice whole-heartedly. Furthermore, he knew many of the bigger retailers in country towns and soon we were adding them to our group. He could plan building alterations and extensions, talk to a builder in his own language and continue his contact to the completion of the job. There was fantastic co-operation between retailers in the conversion to self-service. With any impending opening, the ground work completed, an opening day agreed, special opening offers arranged and delivery times set, our own team would arrive and also five or more of our retailers would help out in their own time – usually late in the evening. A work rota was carefully arranged and the midnight oil burned bright. By the following morning what had been an old fashioned out-of-date counter service shop would be opened as a sparkling new self-service. Pat, or a local celebrity, friend of the family or I would make a little speech to the crowd, cut the tape and away things went. Such marvellous fellowship I will never forget.

I Reach the Top

The weekly bulletin was a useful means of communication in Musgrave and I quote from the copy of the 6 July 1962. "We are pleased to announce that Mr Arthur Creighton has been co-opted to the Board of Musgrave Brothers Ltd. We all know how very hard he has always worked and that the prosperity of our firm is his first consideration. We are sure that all our staff will join us in wishing him continued success in his new position of Sales Director." I was the second person outside the family to join the Board – the other being Alan Wilkie, who had been invited by John L. Musgrave in recognition of his sterling services in helping with financial problems at the time.

There was another appointment of importance also that year, this time affecting Jack Musgrave. Phyllis Goodwin, his late father's secretary who had continued as his, had retired and her successor was Nancy Motherway who had been with the company since May 1942.

Jack made no mistake in his selection of Nancy: apart from being blessed with good looks and an outstanding personality, she was absolutely reliable, capable and a dedicated person.

It is interesting to note that, at that time, we had nine travellers: Finbarr Ormond, Dick O'Dell, Con O'Connell, Willie Livingston, Willie Cavanagh, Robert Barber, Paddy Simpson, Reggie Tracey and Dan Coakley. Eric Gosnel acted as a reserve and he and Paddy Simpson are still with us, in the Cash & Carry at Airport Road, Cork.

Other wholesalers were now beginning to realise that big changes were imminent. When I first introduced the "new religion" some people thought I was crazy and that Irish retailers could never be united. And as for paying cash – well that was impossible. In Cork, M.D. Daly and Jamaica Banana merged to form Munster United Merchants and introduced the Spar symbol. In Dublin, P.E. Barrett, D. Tindell and McNulty & O'Reilly of Bray also united as Amalgamated Wholesalers Ltd., and Looney & Company of Limerick did the same. Punch & Company and Hazletts of Dundalk introduced an English symbol called Mace.

Pat Hickey and I continued to beaver away. We held regular, regional meetings with our retailers at central venues and, by now, were well ahead in the race to secure the more progressive retailers to lay the foundation on which to build for the future.

Finance was a problem as banks were very nervous of lending to independent retailers and there was no Industrial Credit Corporation then. We had to find the cash ourselves and deal within our limits. We sought out desirable situations, purchased premises that we sold back to retailers over an agreed period, made small loans to help conversion and arranged extended credit on opening orders. By now we had also simplified the ordering system by the introduction of the Price List Order Form – PLOF for short. This book contained every item stocked, all priced and showing suggested high and low retail prices. The PLOF was posted to the retailer weekly and he filled in his order and then returned it with a cheque for the previous week's order. Orders were compiled from the book, invoices prepared and a handling charge added, according to the size. Though we did not quite realise it at the time, it was the thin end of the wedge for commercial travellers.

A Happy Home

We really loved Mill House, the spaciousness and comfort of a fine old mansion, the peace and quietness of the countryside and the enjoyment of a fine garden with splendid lawns, shrubberies, a rose garden and a fine kitchen garden, with the added attraction of a beautiful stream meandering under rustic bridges through the grounds. We also had an odd interruption when the local fox-hunters were on the chase. On one such occasion we had a rare opportunity to witness the proverbial cunning of the wily fox.

The hounds were in full chase as they broke over a low wall fringing the cliff, at the edge of the lawn in front of the house, their baying enough to frighten the whole area. They raced frantically up and down, evidently losing the scent, and then, on catching a fresh one, made off over the wall and away up the valley their baying getting fainter and fainter. It was then we caught sight of another movement – lo and behold, from a secret hiding place in the cliff face, Reynard cautiously reappeared by the wall and looked carefully around before making off in the opposite direction. You could almost see the smile on his face!

Our family also enjoyed the old place during school vacations and especially at Christmas; but, in 1963 we had another reason for appreciation. Our eldest girl, Jean, on completing her studies at Trinity in Irish and French and obtaining her degree, had – like so many others at this famous University – met the man of her dreams and fallen in love. He was also a language student and so their wedding day was set for Thursday, 22 August, at 1.00pm in St Luke's Church, St Luke's Cross, Cork. The ceremony was performed by Rev. Canon George Salter and Jean became Mrs. Harold George McAfee. After a sumptuous wedding reception at the Metropole Hotel all were invited to Mill House for the afternoon and the fine setting for such an important event was really appreciated. We were, however, to lose Jean to another country as she and Harry had decided to take up teaching posts in England.

It was not the first such event there as my brother Bill's daughter Rhoda, who had become Mrs Michael Stevenson, on exactly the same day four years earlier, also had had the facility of Mill House.

A Thorough Gentleman

While I attended VG meetings in England regularly, Jack Musgrave also accompanied me to any of the bigger ones when principals of the English wholesalers would be present. Jack and I worked very well together and he was quite an amazingly unpretentious person for a man in his position. On our journeys he always treated me more as a guest than an employee. His courtesy and quiet understanding underlined what a thorough gentleman he was. To demonstrate – Bob van Schaik had organised a conference for all voluntary group traders in Europe to take place in Paris and Jack and I agreed to attend. We ran into problems in London and who arranged an alternative – not I as would normally be expected, but Jack. Miraculously, we caught a boat-train and then the ferry, but no cabins were available. I actually slept in a saloon while a very noisy game of poker went on beside me. Jack selected to try the open deck, but got no sleep at all. Despite this, when we eventually arrived in Paris he insisted on showing me Notre Dame and the Eiffel Tower before the conference started. It was a pleasure to work with him.

As we were in Paris, Jack also availed of the opportunity to visit a prominent wholesaler. I think that, at the back of his mind, he was contemplating arranging training here for his nephew, Hugh Mackeown, whom he knew would soon be joining the company. Hugh's mother, Vivienne, is the late John L. Musgrave's daughter.

The organisation we found at this wholesaler was really outstanding, particularly in the field of fruit and fresh garden produce. The area devoted to this activity consisted of a series of unloading bays, backed by storage space. During the day, the manager compiled his requirements for the next day. These were passed to a man who sat in a high office overlooking everything behind a battery of telephones. Once the outgoing activity was finished, he got busy. He had contacts all over Europe. Some growers produced exclusively for the firm on contract and others were independent, but he knew exactly what range each produced – so it would be tomatoes from Italy, onions from Spain, grapes from the South of France, and so on. He would place his orders which were loaded on lorries immediately and transported through the night to the wholesale depot in Paris. On arrival at the gate, the driver would ring to speak to the controller on a built-in phone. Having been identified, he was informed which number bay to unload at and a button was pressed to allow the gates to open. The lorry drove in, unloaded, and got a receipt. By early morning the bays would be full and ready to be collected by the day's customers.

The Principal of the business also had an amazing filing system of all his customers, not alone the usual business information such as assets, banker, credit worthiness, annual accounts, etc., but also their private lives as well. He had information on a customer's wife, family and his connection and (being French) all about any mistresses – including their telephone numbers – crafty Frenchman!

On 10 October 1965, Hugh Neil Mackeown joined the company. He started, as is usual, right at the bottom, compiling orders and progressed on to warehouse management. A fine tall, good looking, athletic type and a hard worker. And as time was to tell, blessed with the foresight and business acumen of his illustrious grandfather. Only the future would tell how fortunate Musgrave Brothers was in all this.

At Mill House we had yet another wedding to celebrate that year. Our second daughter, Marjorie, having finished her studies at Alexandra College and qualifying as a Froebal Teacher, had caught the same "disease" as her sister and fallen in love with Edward (Ted) Whitaker, a member of a well-known Cork family. The wedding took place at midday on 2 September 1965, and also took place at St Luke's Church with the service conducted by Rev. Canon George Salter. Once again we enjoyed the excellent fare provided by the Metropole Hotel, followed by an afternoon at Mill House. So, now Gladys and I had only Byron at home. He had made up his mind what he wanted to achieve and was studying and working hard to be a Chartered Accountant with a local firm Atkins Chirnside. He was an outstanding hockey player with Garryduff and was selected to play for Munster many times and, at a later date, for Ireland. By then, however, he was in his final year at Accountancy and very wisely, but not without mental agony, had to decide which came first – and so he never gained his hockey cap.

Chapter 13

EXPANSION

On the business front, the endless negotiations with manufacturers continued and intensified. As most of these took place in Dublin, it was decided that we should have an office there. Unfortunately, our good friends Carton Brothers could not agree and decided to pull out of the VG organisation. This was very sad as we worked well together and they were a good company. However, the decision, we felt, was a sound one, so a search for a new "partner" began.

My good friend and colleague, Willie MacBrateney's favourite pastime was playing bridge and, as expected, he was very good at it. Through this activity, at a tournament in Galway, he met Mrs Joan Niland who, having lost her husband, managed the wholesale grocery firm of the same name. Niland's Ltd., were the leading grocers in the West of Ireland, operating out of Galway. In due course, a meeting was arranged between Joan and me. I liked this lady immediately, she was straightforward and intelligent, ran a well managed outfit and was a person of great charm. I made several visits to Galway and in due course, in 1966, Nilands decided to adopt the VG system. They were followed by J. Garvey & Sons of Drogheda in the following year covering the East, and including Dublin.

Our business was now well established, but our warehouse at Cornmarket Street was unable to cope and was literally bursting at the seams. A new warehouse was needed and Jack Musgrave had been looking at various sites for some time. He finally settled on what has turned out to be a fine location, comprising of seven acres at Tramore Road – near Turner's Cross on the southern side of Cork City. Some didn't think much of his choice and said privately and half jokingly that the selection had more to do with its nearness to Kinsale where he lived than any other reason. In fact, he was once again displaying an extraordinary quality that I had so often witnessed in his father – the ability to visualise the future. With today's new road network in place it was a superb choice. Building had been in progress since December 1965 and soon the building was ready for occupation – 6 April was the chosen date. The move was a masterpiece of organisation and everyone, absolutely everyone, had a part to play. A huge fleet of lorries was organised and, with the co-operation of the Gardai, the total stock was safely transported.

The new premises of 71,000 square feet, with high-rise racking, was very impressive and custom built for the fast and efficient job of stocking, compiling and despatching orders. This was greatly helped by the introduction of combi-tainer compilation and coding. We left the Cash & Carry business in Cornmarket Street with much more room to operate and created more space also for the expansion of the tea business "Musgrave Brooke Bond". The Board, at that time, consisted of Mr Stuart Musgrave (Chairman), Mr J. R. Musgrave (Managing Director), Mr S. H. R. Musgrave (Secretary), Mrs V. R. Mackeown (Hugh N. Mackeown's mother), Mr A. A. Wilkie, Mr P. D. Hickey and myself. In October, the official opening was preformed by   the then Minister of Finance, Mr Jack Lynch, later to become An Taoiseach. We had a gathering of overseas visitors including Dr Bob van Schaik (Director General of VeGe Europe), Mr R. A. Branston (Managing Director VG England), and also some of the principals of the VG English wholesales – Mr C. B. Gibson (Gibson's Ltd.), Mr Herbert Philip (Watson & Philip, Scotland), Mr John Bradfield (Harvey Bradfield & Toyer).

A large portion of the warehouse had been adapted into a conference area, complete with stage and seating for the entire staff who numbered approximately one hundred and twenty. There was much speech making and hand clapping and then the champagne flowed. Some of the staff were totally unfamiliar with this beverage and drank it as they would a pint of porter – Murphy, Beamish or perhaps Guinness. The results were quite astonishing. It took some days before some poor fellas returned to normal. As for me, I had my own problems being in charge of the visitors – all of whom I had met at the airport and safely deposited at Tramore Road just five minutes away. The day was rounded off by a dinner at the Metropole Hotel which was then also part of the Musgrave empire and under the capable management of Mr Douglas Vance.

After a luxurious meal, a few of my visitors – Bob van Schaik, Herbert Philip and Barry Gibson, approached me and said they had had enough of champagne and where could they get a "decent" drink. Just up the street from the hotel is a nice little pub called "The Cork Arms", so where better to go. My friends wished to know the local drinks and I informed them that we manufacture the best gin in the world – C.D.C, the most unique Irish Whiskey appropriately named "Paddy", and two very fine stouts – Murphy and Beamish. "We will try the lot," they said and, God help me, we did.

Later that evening, as I left to find my way home (no breathalyser then and a lot less traffic) my three friends were still sitting in the lounge with a plentiful supply of several cases of beer at hand. They were well prepared for a long hard night's drinking. Nevertheless, when I called at 7.30am the following morning to transport them back to the airport, they were finishing off a full Irish breakfast with no ill effects whatsoever. The opening event was a day never to be forgotten.

Another day not to be forgotten by Gladys or me was 31 January 1967, for on that day we became Granny and Grandpa. Our first grandchild was born to Jean and Harry McAfee in Guildford, England, and she was named Sheena Elizabeth. Strange to say, though we were delighted, we didn't feel a day older.

Life is Perpetual Movement
It is said that as each is born, another is called away and this happened as one of my brothers, Albert, died on 12 May in Dublin.

Being in Dublin, my brother Bill missed him most.

With all the pressure and excitement of business, Gladys and I had little time together, except for weekends. She began to find Mill House a bit too big and too lonely, so we agreed to move once again. Gladys began looking at houses and, being a shrewd woman, she also had a definite course of action in mind. She always said to trade up as the family grows and then trade down as it grows smaller, and thereby make good money. We felt we would like to move back to the southside of the city and in Rochestown House she found what appealed, a lovely Queen Anne style residence on one acre of gardens, perched on a hill, with one of the finest views over Loch Mahon on the River Lee and providing a veritable fairyland of lights from the city after dark. We had a tennis court, a small wood, nice orchard and a vegetable garden. Being on a slope, the gardens lent themselves to beautiful landscaping, rockeries, steps and small lawns. Mill House attracted great interest and was sold to the late Senator Mrs Jenny Dowdall, a good friend of the late Eamon de Valera. I believe she had a second bathroom installed and a bedroom suite designed so that the great man could have every comfort when he visited.

One of the problems with moving to a smaller house is how to fit all the furniture and accumulated paraphernalia in your new abode. We certainly had to part with quite a collection, but when we approached our usual auctioneering friend he informed us, to our utter astonishment, that he could not accept anything for auction. He was sorry, but stated that a pact existed between the Cork auctioneers that we would not be accommodated as we had used the Cork office of a Dublin based company to sell our premises. This was true as the manager was a close friend of mine and had helped in finding Rochestown House for us. Now we had a problem.

We decided, eventually, to do the job ourselves and we fixed our own prices for every article, put an advertisement in *The Cork Examiner* and *Evening Echo* and that was that. The results were phenomenal. Gladys rang me one day and told me to come home immediately. When I arrived I could not even drive up my own avenue with the amount of cars. It was a huge crowd that she, Byron and I had to cope with and at the end of the day the tally far exceeded our best expectations. It must have been one of the most rewarding incidents in our lives for the good sale was only the cream on the milk.

The profit we made on the sale of the house paid in full for the purchase of Rochestown House. My wife's shrewd planning had paid off handsomely.

This was certainly a very eventful year, both privately and in business. On the business side, in February we fulfilled a long sought necessity when we opened a Central Office at 3, Dartmoor Square, in Dublin. The function of this would be to negotiate long-term agreements and special offers with manufacturers and develop our ever growing "own brand" range. We duly managed to find and appoint a new manager whose name was Bruce Carswell. He was a young Belfast man of 29 years and was educated at Campbell and Queens University. Bruce had five years experience of the grocery trade with J & J Hazlett Limited in Belfast and then was in marketing with Aspro-Nicholas. The official title was "VG Grocery Services Limited" and our group was now national with Nilands Limited of Galway and J. Garvey & Sons of Drogheda.

Musgrave Matters

When we started, our retail members simply displayed an electric sign in their window to identify themselves. This stated "VG Services". This was very inadequate and also presented problems, as it was part of their lighting system and difficult to remove if, as sometimes happened, a member proved unsatisfactory. We now had illuminated facias with the VG symbol (a wedge of blue with the letters in yellow) and the title "Foodmarket". This was a great improvement, but still presented similar problems. Though it would be easy to remove the sign, as it was the property of the member and he had to pay for it, his permission was necessary. We were not smart enough yet to realise, as we did many years later, that the best way was for the wholesaler to supply the facia free of charge and thus maintain full control in every eventuality.

Jack Musgrave was Chairman of VG Grocery Services Limited and as he and I travelled to regular meetings we had much to discuss and made good use of our time. In August 1967, further structural changes took place in Musgrave Brothers.

The first Mr Stuart Musgrave, a founder member of the company, had passed away on 3 December 1934. His son, also named Stuart, had been Company Secretary since 1937 until his appointment as Chairman on 22 November 1955. This was the same date that his son, Hugh, was appointed Secretary and that Jack Musgrave was appointed Managing Director. I had been appointed Marketing Director in 1965.

Now, Stuart was resigning as Chairman and Jack Musgrave was taking over that office. Hugh became Vice-Chairman on resigning as Secretary and that office was taken up by Mr F.W. Markham – who had recently joined the company from Beamish & Crawford Ltd. Also on that date, Hugh N. Mackeown became a Director.

As our business grew, so our organisation had to change. I had long realised that our retailers and our own wholesale business had to operate as one unit, indeed, as if we were one big company under the same management.

Musgrave Brothers, however, was a privately owned wholesale company operating the VG system with over one hundred privately owned retailers, something the public found a bit difficult to understand, despite numerous explanations. From our earliest associations, I knew we had to understand retailers' needs and problems, so I had divided up the area we serviced into three regions and appointed the three best men I had to service them. Their job was to guide the retailers in their decisions and to help them with any problems that might arise. These men were Jim O'Donovan, Reggie Treacy and Dick O'Dell. However, only one had any retail experience and that was the latter, who had worked in his own family business in Dromcollogher and now he informed me that he had accepted a job with Cork Distillers and was leaving. I determined that he would have to be replaced by a man with first hand self-service knowledge. My final selection was a young man called Seamus Scally, who was managing a supermarket in Dublin for the Five Star group. To facilitate him, I arranged our meeting to coincide with a retail meeting in the Newpark Hotel, Kilkenny. I immediately liked this man as he was straightforward, business like and knew all the answers to the various rigorous question I flung at him. He got the job!

Little did I know then what a jewel I had unearthed, and how much this appointment would mean to the company in later years. Seamus soon proved his abilities. He understood the supermarket business and had that very valuable talent of "thinking retail". His advice, especially to those going into self-service, was really invaluable. Now, we were really starting to move forward and I was so busy I hardly had time to think much about myself, but I was not feeling in the best of form and was making frequent visits to my doctor. Things came to a head in May 1968 when, after X-rays, gallstones were discovered and I underwent surgery in the Bons Secours Hospital on 30 May. Though very successful, it is a serious operation and it was well into July before I could resume work.

On 21 June 1968, VG Grocery Services was incorporated and, in September, we added a marketing manager to our central office staff. This was a man with wide retail experience in Vancouver, Canada, and who was soon to be well known in the food distribution business here. His name was Tim Nolan.

Amsterdam

To gain publicity and at the same time help a deserving cause, I had organised a VG dinner dance each year, the highlight of which was to select an attractive young lady and crown her "Miss VG" for that year. The function became one of the highlights of Cork's social calendar and we always had a local TD, Lord Mayor or some such celebrity honouring us with his or her presence. Musgrave Brothers also had, for many years, held a Christmas dinner dance for all the staff. Both functions, needless to say, were held in the Metropole Hotel.

The Musgrave event of 1968 was the scene for a very tragic event that left its mark on many of us for a long time. Retired staff were always invited, as they still are today, and amongst them was John Musgrave's previous secretary, Phyllis Goodwin. She, to all appearances, was in her usual cheerful and lively good form. To the utter shock of all, during a dance she suffered a heart attack and had passed away before we could get her to hospital. Personally, I was very upset as she was an old friend and I had only been danc-ing with her twenty minutes earlier. Surely a stark reminder of the fact that in the midst of life we are in death.

Every few years Dick Branston's English central office organised visits to various European countries and always reserved a number of places for VG Ireland. These events usually lasted a week and were very valuable as we saw, first hand, how supermarkets were developing. We always had a conference at which a prominent speaker would outline what lay ahead. It also afforded me with an opportunity to get to know my own retailers better and vice versa.

Shortly after introducing the VG system in 1960, we had invited Bob van Schaik to visit. In the following year he did so and made a very impressive address to our pioneers about VeGe on the Continent and how it had developed. I recollect taking Bob on a tour of West Cork and, to our utter astonishment, he had a great knowledge of local history, especially that of Timoleague and its Abbey. Another astonishment was in store for us. Having a few pre-luncheon drinks at a well-known hotel in a well-known town (no names – no pack drill, as they say in the army) and knowing Bob was used to Dutch geneva gin and his poor regard for our own C.D.C., I put a word in the proprietor's ear and Bob got a glass of the finest local brew of Poitin. He took a small sip and then draining his glass he held it out to me and said, "That was wonderful Arthur, please get me another".

Together with a party of our retailers, we paid a reciprocal visit to Amsterdam in 1964 to celebrate VeGe's thirtieth birthday. This was a splendid trip but not without its moments. One of our retailers had never been out of Ireland and his wife, who did not accompany us, implored me to take good care of her Sean. I did not know that she had good reasons for her request as "her Sean" really took some looking after! He was scared stiff of flying and it took quite a few brandies before we could get him aboard for London! In Amsterdam one evening, on our way back to our hotel we found ourselves in a very quiet street, but soon the silence was broken by the call of a nightingale. On tracing the sound, our eyes were led upwards to brightly lit windows where ladies were beckoning. We were in one of Amsterdam's notorious red light districts – but not for long. A police car pulled up alongside us and informed us that we were not welcome in such a dangerous place and quickly escorted us away.

Another memorable occasion was when we sailed down the river Rhine in 1967. It was an unforgettable kaleidoscope of fairyland castles perched high on crags above the mighty river with its ever changing traffic of barges, boats and ships. We visited the famous Rhine Falls and had a night never to be forgotten at Rudesheim, where we had anchored. In the town that evening there was a novelty on sale that consisted of a battery that fitted in your breast pocket connected to a coloured light that you attached to your coat lapel, and this light kept flashing. It was an unforgettable sight to see a long chain of bobbing lights weaving their way along the river bank to our ship all singing "We all live in a Yellow Submarine...". Back on board we found that the bar was locked and on arousing the Purser he, very unwisely, gave us the key. Someone concocted a "Devil's Brew" in an ice bucket, Pat O'Shea of Cobh sat down at the piano and Arthur Creighton started to sing. We had a fantastic concert, but for several days later I could only whisper due to overextending my vocal cords on the top notes of "Danny Boy".

How to Mix Business and Fun

In 1970 we embarked on another wonderful event known as the "Adriatic Conference" held on board the cruise ship *S.S. Fiorita*. We flew from Gatwick to Venice and as our flight was delayed by three or four hours we all got complimentary drink and ten minutes to visit the pilot in the cockpit. My turn came as we flew over Switzerland and what an unforgettable panorama unfolded below. The following day, as we did not board the ship until 5.30 pm, we had the morning free and I took our party on a tour of the famous city with which I was quite well acquainted.

At St Mark's Square we visited the famous Cathedral and all attended Mass – two Methodists, two Church of Ireland and four Roman Catholics – a real ecumenical octet. On emerging onto the famous square we heard a commotion at a fruit-vending stand, only to discover that two of our party were lending a helping hand to the fruit seller, much to his dislike, and he was proclaiming this in a vociferous outpouring of Italian. It was just as well that we didn't understand what he was saying, but it cost us a few thousand lira to sort that one out!

Returning to our hotel, we called at a nearby bar and none of the party knew what to ask for, so, after a quiet chat with the barmaid, beautiful, tall, cut glass tumblers were soon presented and all declared the drink delicious. But what was it? Whatever it was my good friend, the late John Riordan of Rathcormack, and I found ourselves way past the hotel having great difficulty in relocating it. It took a good lunch to sober us up, but to this day I am still asked what the concoction was. As a souvenir we all bought the glasses and I sometimes look at mine as it winks at me from the cabinet while I enjoy a quiet smile. You see, I had a great friend in the late Bill Oakley of Cork Distillers who taught me how to mix'em.

As we cruised towards Split we had a conference on Monday

under the chairmanship of E. G. Bradley (Chairman of VG England) and the speakers were Mr K. van Musschenbrock and Ms Sheila Black, both of *The Financial Times*. We reached Split in the afternoon and after a brief guided tour we set off for Kator – a charming old town but nothing compared with the mediaeval splendour of Dubrovnik, where we berthed for the night. That cruise will always be memorable for me as I shared a table with one of my best friends, John Riordan, and his charming wife Pru. John was the sort of man one only meets once in a lifetime, a real gem, and fabulously good company, but unfortunately he is no longer with us.

We crossed the Adriatic to Ancona on Tuesday night. John J. Harold (another friend of mine from Newcastlewest) and I had selected one-berth cabins which were situated right in the bow and what a storm we had to plough through. There was only a steel bulk-head between us and the tempest, so we were very glad to reach port. Strange to say, it was not the last I saw of the *S.S. Fiorita*. Some years later, Gladys and I were in Bulgaria on holiday and took a short cruise on the Black Sea to Istanbul. To my surprise, when we berthed, there alongside was the familiar vessel.

I ventured aboard, identified myself, was offered a welcome drink and learned that she was now on charter between Istanbul and the Greek Islands. She was a beautiful ship.

More Expansion and Computerisation

Back in the business we were on the move again, this time opening a Cash & Carry in Limerick in 1969. In Group Trading, as we developed it became apparent that, despite all the activity, it was clear that one style of marketing did not suit all. Many of our members had expanded and in those days 1,000 square feet was considered a big shop. The style of business they did and its needs were quite different from the smaller outlets. The answer seemed to lie in a second Group, aimed at the "Convenience Shop" sector of the trade – and we called this "Shoprite".

During all this, Gladys and I had two more grandchildren added to our brood. Julie Carina Whitaker was born on 14 May 1968 and Rebecca Jane McAfee was born on 23 January 1969. And we still did not feel any older!

On 9 June 1970, we formed a new central office company which we called "Irish Modern Distributors Limited" or "IMD", that had two subsidiary companies, "VG Services Limited" and "Trade Markets Limited (Cash & Carry Division)". Mr Jack Musgrave was Chairman of IMD and I was appointed the first Chairman of the VG Services symbol group.

Coming home to Cork on the train that evening Jack and I were discussing the catering trade. Whilst we always traded with hotels and restaurants, it only represented a very small part of our business and we knew that there was much more business to be had.

I had had several meetings with friendly hotel proprietors and Hugh Mackeown and I had recently returned from a visit to Watson & Philip of Glasgow, who operated a very profitable and extremely well organised catering division. We now knew enough about it to realise that it differed so much from conventional distribution that it required a separate division to be successful and we were contemplating the idea of how to start such a venture. The most successful company in this field in Cork was Smith's Stores, who also operated a high class grocery and provisions shop in Patrick's Street and another on the Douglas Road.

Quite suddenly an idea entered my head, it would be a terrific and costly fight to wrestle business from them, so if you can't beat them, join them! I revealed my thoughts to Jack and his eyes lit up, "What a splendid idea Arthur!" he said. "Of course, we should have thought of it long ago, I will get busy right away". And he did.

Discussions took place with the two Smith brothers who ran the business – Ronnie and his half-brother John. In due course the merger was agreed. John was, by far, the keener businessman of the two and made sure we didn't buy cheaply, but, as I said to my fellow Board members, we were getting more than a company, we were getting two good businessmen also. It is interesting to note that John Smith told me many years later that he had only agreed to join Musgrave Brothers until he formed new plans, but he had found us so good to work with that he decided to stay on. Once again, we were adding great strength to our team.

This was also the year that the company entered into the computer age, as we joined a service used by some 12 English wholesalers operated by a company in Manchester under the title of "Discus".

We had preliminary talks with them and it was agreed that a direct telephone line would be set up and in due course we would introduce sales analysis, gross profit analysis, stock control and recommended re-order levels. We had also got into the bacon and egg business and operated as Musgrave Provisions from Tramore Road. Amongst many good things I learned from working with Jack Musgrave was the importance of listening. Jack was a good speaker but even a better listener, and it is rightly said that it is as difficult to learn to be a good listener as to become a good violinist! However, listening can create problems if it helps invoke sympathy, especially if you are like Jack was and love to help people to expand and succeed.

The Tramore Road warehouse was built under the direction of a friend of Jack's, Carl Campbell, who was a qualified engineer. We started a new company called "Creative Stores Construction" under Carl's management. We still had the Metropole Hotel and Musgrave Brothers (Sweets) Limited, both old established businesses and, in addition, we had Musgrave Provisions, Musgrave Shop Fittings and Embassy Caterers. We had a jointly owned tea business, Musgrave Brooke Bond, another jointly owned business, Kinsale Eggs, and an interest in Catering Foods in Macroom. Our latest addition was Smith's Stores.

I sat on the Boards of some of these companies and it was very time consuming. I often felt that we would have been better occupied just running our main business of food distribution. Over the course of time others saw likewise and Creative Stores was sold to Carl Campbell, the egg business was discontinued, as was Shop Fittings, and Provisions and Frozen Foods were bought out by management.

During 1970 also, I lost a very good colleague and friend with the death of Willie MacBrateney who had served the company so well for 38 years. His reputation as a food buyer was second to none in Ireland and his sympathetic understanding and willingness to help others was legendary. I missed Willie greatly, not alone as a good friend but as an outstanding fellow worker and I will never forget his outstanding contribution when starting to build our group.

John and Ronnie Smith also lost their father, W.J. Foster-Smith, whose great business acumen had built the Smith's Stores business.

We Tidy Up!

Hugh Mackeown was now appointed joint Managing Director but he still retained responsibility for both warehouse and transport, Cash & Carry division, and for stores. For some time we had been operating a number of retail supermarkets owned by our own company. These were situated (under the name of "Joint Ventures") at Togher in Cork, Food Fair in Dungarvan, Magennis Supermarkets 1968 Limited in Kilkenny, Jack's Stores in Charleville and in Bishopstown and Smith's Stores in Patrick's Street and in Douglas Road, Cork. Some of our retail members were not enamoured with this idea and over the course of time it was decided, and rightly so, that we would be better specialising in that which we did well, i.e. wholesale distribution, so we sold most of these stores to their management and discontinued the others.

In addition to being very good at business, Hugh Mackeown was also very good at golf and sailing and a leader in both – especially in golf where he went on to play for Ireland. Jack Musgrave was also a keen sailing enthusiast but loved horses and hunted with South Union.

Paddy Simpson was now managing the Cash & Carry in Cornmarket Street and his assistant was Eric Gosnell. We had a new appointment of Public Relations Officer – he was Noel Murphy, better known for his prowess in rugby as he was capped for Ireland many times. It so happens that the well-known home of Dolphin Rugby Club, called Musgrave Park, is actually across the road from Musgrave's distribution warehouse in Tramore Road. Many think that there is a financial connection, however, the only connection is the name as Musgrave Park was named after Jimmy Musgrave (John's brother), who was a great enthusiast and one time president of the Irish Rugby Football Union and past president of Constitution Rugby Club. Neither John nor his other brother Willie (who managed the Metropole Hotel) had any interest in this sport whatsoever.

By now I had appointed two men, Mitchell Barry and Harry McAfee (my son-in-law, who had become disillusioned with teaching and banking in England and decided to return to Ireland). Mitchell graduated to Musgrave Provisions and became General Manager and eventually, when the company was sold off to management, became Managing Director of the renamed company "Allied Foods".

Another generation of the Musgrave family also joined the company with the arrival of Peter J. Musgrave (son of Jack). Gladys and I also had "new arrivals", another grandchild and this time it was a boy named Simon Edward Whitaker on the 20 August 1970.

Ten Great Years of Progress

It was now over ten years since we had first started our group of independent retailers under the VG symbol and set out on the long and eventful voyage of discovery of a new and better way to do business and serve the public together. The first three or four years had been extremely difficult and sometimes frustrating and I often said to Gladys that if it didn't improve soon that I would call it a day. But with the great support of our better members and our own good team in the business we were now going very well and the future looked bright. Perhaps our achievements are best outlined in my own contribution to a celebratory tenth anniversary brochure produced to mark that event. The following is what I said:

"As we celebrate our tenth year under our VG symbol, I congratulate all members on such an outstanding achievement. Starting literally from scratch in 1960, together we have welded all the loose individual operations that formed the old pattern of food distribution into a modern, streamlined, low cost marketing organisation taking its rightful place as leader in this country.

"Members will remember the pattern before we introduced Voluntary Group Trading. Manufacturers sold to wholesalers and apart from producing showcards and an odd newspaper advertisement, that is as far as marketing went. Wholesalers sold to retailers and it was left to the retailer alone to get on with the job of selling from there on. Credit was widespread and there was no such thing as self-service. It was up to the ability of each retailer to do the best he could. Because he bought piece-meal, from as many as thirty or forty suppliers, retail costs were high and so were the costs of his wholesalers because of this. Whilst the common aim was to sell as much as possible, each sector – manufacturers, wholesaler and retailer – operated as separate units and there was no means of uniting all three.

"Voluntary Group Trading, and in particular our Group, because we pioneered the system in Ireland, changed all this. We introduced a system and organisation and with your co-operation, application and hard work and the co-operation of the manufacturers, we produced the machine that efficiently moves thousands of pounds worth of goods every day from manufacturer to consumer at a much lower cost then was possible previously. We have made possible national advertising and mass display of the product at the same time and, with our organised promotional programme, have produced increases in sales of quantities quite impossible under the old system. We have brought modern well organised shopping facilities to the furthest corners of the country, for we pioneered self-service and the Supermarket here. We have, in addition, brought a much wider range of goods at keener prices then was possible before to the Irish housewife.

"As we stand on the threshold of the seventies, we all can be proud of what we have accomplished together. We can look forward, with confidence, to the constant challenge of an ever changing trade, sure in the knowledge that closer co-operation, sound constructive thinking and hard endeavour will stand us well as it has in the last ten wonderful years we now celebrate together."

In the same brochure Bruce Carswell compared the four years, 1967 to 1971. From 242 members we now moved to 292 and turnover had increased from eight million to fourteen million pounds. Total square footage doubled to 246,500 square feet, with an average of 845 square feet and 88per cent were self-service. Rightly he forecast an even more dramatic next decade, with out-of-town shopping centres, huge car parks and a stronger presence in Dublin City. He also rightly forecast standard decor and layout and also standard systems and procedures. Bob van Schaik, recalling his first visit in 1961, congratulated us on our progress and put us "Top of the rank among all the European Voluntary Trading groups". Richard (Dick) Branston said, "To-day, in relative terms. VG in the Republic of Ireland is even more successful than in the United Kingdom with a higher proportion of self-service shops and a larger slice of its own market".

Our Chairman, Jack Musgrave, said:

> It was most satisfactory to look back on the past ten years and to see how VG has gone from strength to strength. When VG introduced group trading to Ireland in 1960 it was considered to be a most foolish thing to do and certainly, to the traditional retail of those days, it did seem a most revolutionary move.
>
> However, in the past ten years VG has become a household word and has taken a prominent place in the Irish retail scene. That this has happened is entirely due to team-work plus hard work – both at wholesale and retail levels.

The team-work at wholesale level has been between three separate wholesale companies, under separate Irish ownership who have come together to develop VG as a completely national group. The liaison between the three wholesalers has been magnificent, and all three have benefited from the experience of the others.

The team-work between the wholesaler and retailers has been even more remarkable. Ten years ago an independent retailer viewed his wholesaler with suspicion, but today the VG retailer knows that he and his VG wholesaler are partners in the modern chain of distribution. He also knows that his VG wholesaler is totally committed to helping him to expand and prosper. He knows that what is good for the one is good for the other.

I would like to pay tribute to all my colleagues in all three wholesale companies and to the 292 VG retailers, who together have shown that voluntary co-operation has a tremendous potential, and has an even bigger role to play in the future in distributing food throughout Ireland.

There were also contributions from Louis Garvey who stated the dramatic effect that joining VG had on his business – doubling turn-over in four years and reorganising their way of doing business – and expressed great confidence in the future. There was praise from Nilands for their retailers for their large investment in modernising their stores, demonstrating in the best way possible their confidence in the VG system. Dan Griffin also mentioned Niland's great confidence and the purchase of a twelve acre site and the erection of a modern distribution warehouse was proof of that. (He also spoke for all three wholesalers on our two years preparation for the establishment of decimal trading on 14 February of that year.)

There was also a tribute from a few enlightened manufacturers who were beginning to realise that voluntary group trading was here to stay and old ways of doing business were being revolutionised.

There followed a list of the 292 retailers, it is interesting to note that a large proportion have expanded and prospered and continue to provide a service to the public that is second to none.

We Move Into Dublin

We were now well established and well ahead of other symbol groups, but there was much more to be done before we could take on the multiples, as we knew we must. Hugh Mackeown was now Managing Director and Jack Musgrave was Chairman. In Hugh, we encountered a very different style of management, more forceful, outgoing and authoritarian in style. He very much liked to give more freedom to management and let them make their own decisions, provided they delivered good results. In so many ways, as I often said to him, he had much of his grandfather, John L. Musgrave, in his genes.

We were now the only wholesale grocer in Ireland using the computer service. We commenced strictly with the grocery part of our business and soon saw much improved service levels and lower stockholding days. We were preparing the general merchandise (hardware and drapery) for inclusion by January 1972 and aimed to commence recording daily sales by 18 January.

For quite a few years we had been looking at the Dublin market, the biggest single market in which we had no presence. Now, the decision had been made that Musgrave would enter by means of the Cash & Carry operation and the man selected to direct this was Pat Hickey. As Pat said at the time, "We have always wanted our share of the Dublin market, but we waited until the radical new developments which were convoluting had stabilised. For example the prophets of doom chanted incessantly that the small independent retailer had no future. We believed otherwise. Now time has proved us correct and as a result, the big developments in trading patterns will be the use of Cash & Carry warehouses."

This project would be quite different from anything the trade had encountered previously, at a massive eighty-five thousand square feet and involving an investment of approximately three quarters of a million pounds. It was to be situated in Robinhood Industrial Estate and would carry, besides a full range of groceries, a very extensive range of non-food lines in hardware, electrical goods, paints, home decorating products, wines and spirits, stationery, gardening products and frozen foods. In entering Dublin, Jack Musgrave achieved a life-long ambition of not just getting into the Dublin market but of getting a better deal for the wholesalers.

Jack Musgrave claimed that nowhere in the world were wholesale margins so low and he fought hard, as did we all, against the unfair terms manufacturers imposed by direct trading with retailers. He was now about to create the opportunity to finally convince manufacturers that the economies of scale in this new venture would substantially reduce the costs of distribution.

As far as I, personally, was concerned I was about to lose another colleague as Pat Hickey would have to live in Dublin. He and I had worked together for over ten years and understood each other so well that we often didn't need to plan or discuss how to proceed, as each knew exactly how the other was thinking. It was a great pleasure to work with him. He had a brilliant, far seeing intelligence, almost psychic at times. He was a tremendous worker, possessed a fine sense of humour and had a great cant that often relieved the stress and strain of long hours.

We soldiered together all over the South of Ireland, obtaining new members, helping others to operate more profitably, others to expand or buy new premises, addressing numerous meeting and working outrageously long hours. Success is a tremendous stimulant and we certainly were successful. Now Pat had the new title of "Development Director" and I knew that I would miss him. Our retailers gave him a splendid farewell dinner at the Metropole Hotel and presented him with a colour television (something quite special then) and wished him every success.

We had survived a bank strike and an investigation by the Fair Trade Commission and now we had a huge new venture on our hands. Robinhood commenced trading in the Spring of 1972 and the tape was cut by the Chairman's wife, Mrs Molly Musgrave. It was an immediate success and has continued so to this day.

In Tramore Road I had appointed a new buyer who was with United Merchants (Spar), called Noel Hanley and I had moved Seamus Scally up to VG Manager and Terence Murphy, who had been with us for some time, was Manager for Shoprite. We also had a new Office Manager in Frank Walley. The latter was the fastest man we ever had – that is at running in athletics – he accumulated the Munster Championship 100 metres, County Championship 100 metres, 100 yards and 220, 300 and 440 metres. He had also represented Ireland in athletics against Iceland. In golf, Hugh Mackeown was selected for the Cork Golf Club Irish Senior Team and Jack Musgrave came second in his Dragon class yacht *Wolfhound* in the Edinburgh Cup.

CHAPTER 14

OFF TO THE USA

For some time Pat Hickey, Hugh Mackeown and I had been contemplating a visit to the USA. Pat had been before and, as things worked out, could not make the second visit. So, Hugh and I set off from Shannon on 14 April 1971 – our first stop New York. I nearly missed it also as I had caught a dreadful dose of 'flu and was kept going with antibiotics. It is interesting now, over 20 years later, to read what I said to the Annual Conference about the visit.

In April, Hugh Mackeown and I visited the USA. Our object was to meet people in our own trade, find out as much as we could on their side of the market, how Voluntary Group Trading was faring, what were present trends in general and in non-foods in particular and, of course, to see the country.

In the space of three weeks or so, we visited New York, Dayton Ohio, took a flying visit to Pittsburgh and Lexington in Ohio, spent quite some time in Chicago, Minneapolis and St. Paul, then right across to the West Coast to visit one of the largest distributors in the world – Certified Grocers of California, with a warehouse covering no less than fifteen acres, and then flew back in one hop over the Pole to London and so home to Cork. We spoke to executives of trade associations, voluntary groups, wholesale distributors, manufacturers, chain retailers and independent retailers, shop assistants and people at various levels in between. We covered some sixteen thousand miles, slept very little, ate too much and picked up a lot of useful information and know how.

My first impression of the States was that of bigness or magnitude – the magnitude of everything and people of every sort, class and colour; buildings – immense sky scrapers or high-rise as they were then called; roads – five lanes each way running hundreds of miles, everywhere cars by the million (two for every three persons in Los Angeles); conference halls – like playing field; planes – operating as frequently and easily as bus services; shopping centres – like towns; stores – like warehouses. And the magnitude of other things, such as problems of race and colour, crime and drugs; depressed areas; pollution; labour and student unrest; dying railways and down-town shopping. This magnitude makes it very difficult to compare with conditions and living in Ireland. To cope with this magnitude in everything, the American way of life must be well organised. There are right ways and wrong ways of doing every exercise and if you do something the wrong way you will be told, in no uncertain fashion, regardless of who you are or where you are. This is often construed as American rudeness.

Organisation requires training and I found business people there extremely well trained. They work out the correct procedure to perform a job efficiently and that is the only way it is done, and the staff are trained to do it that way only. All right, it can kill individualism but it does get things done correctly.

At present, the American way of life was under enormous strain and in talking to Americans there was evident uncertainty in the future. Fear is there – fear of the colour problem, the drug problem and the economic problems and social problems loom so big. In the cities you do not walk alone at night and parks and quiet streets were to be avoided if one was to keep one's wallet or even one's life. Taxis have bullet-proof glass between driver and fare and had built-in safes to keep the money in, the driver did not have the key and this was stated in bold print on the cab! Drug addiction requires cash to buy drugs and, as some addicts could not work, they steal and rob.

In the suburbs and smaller cities and towns, life goes on much as here and the facilities for good living were everywhere. Huge markets, high wages, huge recreational areas, luxurious clubs and sport centres, all sort of amusements, cultural centres and educational facilities and fantastic means of communication.

They have a clever device in Chicago. There is a ten lane highway running along the lake shore. The division of the traffic lanes is provided by hydraulically operated road blocks. In the morning the controller presses the button and the blocks rise to form a kerb providing eight lanes into town and two out – in the evening, or as traffic warrants, this was changed to eight out and two in. This is an example of American organisation.

From a hotel bedroom telephone you can dial anywhere in America direct. You could also dial direct all the various hotel services including an early morning call – completely automatic. There are so many cars and such excellent roads that public transport is being choked to death. The railways are dying, local bus services are dead, there is no public transport from the airport to town, but the taxi business was huge. Television is mostly colour and there is no licence fee as all stations were financed by commercials – you get plenty of them. "Tele" watching still is a national pastime, people don't go out at night except by car.

So much for general impressions, but what about the Food Trade? What is happening there that may well happen here. What lessons are to be learnt so that we all can avoid pitfalls and losses? America is in the grip of inflation as we are and, in addition, they have suffered a recession so we found the scene very cost conscious. What they call the "Discount Supermarkets" is becoming more and more popular. Discounting is another name for price cutting – with a difference. American discount supermarkets do not give stamps. Again, they tell you so: "No Stamps here - you'll get them at the Post Office!". They don't go in for games or gimmicks: "Go to the Sports Centre if you want games – we don't play them here!" They stock well-known merchandise and a controlled range.

There are also Self-Service Discount Department Stores –these are giants of one hundred thousand square foot with, say, twenty thousand square foot for food. Perishables, for the most part, were not cut in price, the retailer relying on meat, fresh produce and non-foods to maintain his margin. The big chains are building more and more of these discount supermarkets and department stores and their share of the market increased by 10.4% last year compared with 6% for the independents. This in itself is significant.

The tendency is more and more for the very large shopping

areas under one roof offering a wider range of goods, all sold self-service. There is, therefore, greater emphasis on lines other than food, which the Americans call general merchandise. So here, straight away, we found our thinking right in line with theirs. At the other end of the scale, the smaller self-service shop was also coming into its own again – what they call "Convenience Stores" and these registered a sizeable gain of 24% on previous years. The reason is, and it is important, that as stores get larger and larger, people tend to do a mass shop once a week only or less and fill up for other items as the need arises from the Convenience Stores – which is local and quicker. The fact that they pay quite a bit more is outweighed by the saving in time. The middle sector of the trade, those who were not geared big enough for this particular market then are those now facing serious problems.

Coupled with this, the emphasis on good merchandising is tremendous. Merchandising in America is studied in great detail and consumer's habits and how they think and act are under regular review.

As a result their display work has to be seen to be believed. Fittings are tailor made for clear communication, goods are grouped for more and more convenience while shopping and everything is done to take the worry out of shopping but at the same time to induce the shopper to buy more. So it is arranged that as one bought baby food, a comprehensive range of other baby needs is also offered and so on. This is something that we believe is extremely important and we are, at present, experimenting and working on new methods of selling non-foods which we will be presenting to you in the year ahead.

Of course, when one visits the States and sees the vastness of everything and the perfection of their achievements, one asks oneself – How do they do it? The big advantage they have lies in computerisation. A computer produces necessary and important information about business accurately and at a speed quite unbelievable. So the American businessman has, at his fingertips, up-to-the-minute information on how his business is going all the time and he acts constantly to keep it profitable. Trends are also followed closely, selling space is measured according to sales by item and lines that don't sell fast enough are discarded.

Retail prices are determined by the rate of sale and the overall margin required from that particular section. If an item sells fast, the computer reduces the retail price and if is sells slower it increases it. Check-outs linked to computers are being introduced, giving instantaneous and automatic stock control and automatic re-ordering at retail level. All their accounting is done by computer at all levels. There is a flow of information always available on how the customers spend their dollars, by category, on retail prices, on sales per employee, sales per square foot and so on – someone, somewhere is always conducting studies and trades are well organised and there are trade associations for all branches of the trade.

We visited all sorts of supermarkets and stores, from the giants of Self-Service Discount Department Stores and Discount Supermarkets, right through to independent supermarket group members and Convenience Stores. The message there is much as here – the operator who studies the market and supplies its needs is successful. The difference is that the American is very thorough in getting information, has plenty of access to information and is not afraid to act on it.

Their attention to detail is one of the factors that bring success. They are prepared to change with the times.

The voluntary groups are still very strong and the services they provide for their members are very wide and once again very thorough. They organise promotions much as we do, advertising, please note, always in newspapers. They provide handbills, but these are news-sheet size and in colour. They provide advice on expansion or development and on lay-out as we do and they provide a G.P.C. system as we do – but this is computerised. Beyond this, they provide a complete auditing service for their members producing quarterly profit and loss accounts and year-end full results. In addition, they employ specialists for each department of the supermarket who work out and present, down to the smallest detail, how to operate that department plus a full marketing programme. They have a Fresh Meat Programme, a

Dairy Cabinet Programme, one for the Bakery Department, Fresh Produce, Health and Beauty, General Merchandise and Frozen Foods. They provide financial counsellors who guide and advise on financial problems, gave profit and loss account analysis, balance sheet analysis and retail accounting procedures.

They also advise on computer programming and leasing and financial prospectus preparation. You name it, they have it.

Their policy is important – prices are kept as low as possible, all services are charged for separately and demand is such that the service was sufficient to justify them.

Wholesale warehouses are much the same as here – only bigger. We found a very nice little one in California, covering only eighteen acres – all under one roof. Full utilisation of space is of paramount importance to keeping down costs. All voluntary group retailers buy all their needs from their wholesaler, very often fresh meat and fresh produce as well as dry groceries. American retailers are realists, they know they must provide full buying support in order to get low cost distribution. So the warehouses work around the clock – goods start coming in at 8.00 am and this continues until 4.00 pm. The productivity starts then and continues in two shifts until 6.00 am. The sweepers and cleaners come in then and it all starts again at 8.00 am.

Of course, many industries in America work around the clock and, to satisfy the demand of their market, so do some retailers. We found an independent retailer in Dayton Ohio, called Mr Woody, operating a twenty-one thousand square foot supermarket/drug store, plus a fifteen thousand square foot restaurant that seated three hundred and fifty. That supermarket remained open twenty-four hours a day, seven days a week, three hundred and sixty five days a year! Incidentally, he started out as a pedlar with a small truck in 1944!

What then is the message from America? Can you compare activities in a country of three hundred and twenty-seven million people to one with three million? Can we adapt what they do well to suit our needs here? Well, this is what we have been working hard at since we came home. It is not a straight and easy path. We believe, and always did, in moving with the times, we always preached "Get big". The new message is "Get big where the market is big" and where you can dominate it and if you can't do this, specialise – remember the Convenience Store.

The car is king in America and will be here. We must, therefore, never lose sight of this and how it will reflect on our business now and in the future.

We are the first wholesaler in Ireland to computerise our internal system. This is the start of what must grow and grow until we will have all our accounting and management control figures computerised and the same applies to the retail scene. Up to now, we offered a manually operated G.P.C. system to you. Very soon we will offer you a partially computer controlled G.P.C. system, providing a gross profit figure for each PLOF invoice automatically plus the individual gross profit on each commodity group and line you buy, thus providing you with an up-to-the- minute guide to your pricing policy.

We also found that in two aspects we were actually ahead in our thinking. American Cash and Carries are nowhere as good as ours and American wholesalers are only now moving into non-foods or general merchandise. We have already worked out a complete programme for non-foods and will be offering this new scheme to you in the new year. It is a big programme and will take time and participants' full co-operation to get it off the ground, but we are confident that it would produce much bigger sales of general merchandise and a much needed better profit mix in these times of ever rapidly rising costs. We are studying many other better ways of doing things and providing new services for you.

Because of the detailed nature of these and the problems of adapting to our specific needs, they will not occur overnight. We see the possibility in full accounting services and special programmes more closely linked with manufacturers, but it is not possible at this stage to be more specific until we see further. We definitely must try to train our staff to a much higher degree of efficiency and are, at present, looking for a Training Officer. Retail training also must be provided. If we are to come up to European standards we must all become more efficient – we don't pay half enough attention to training and this must be improved. In providing services we must appreciate that good services cost money and we must be prepared to pay for them if we want them.

We see in our group a tremendous potential for the future if we all continue to work even closer together and support each other in every possible way. We must realise, however, that our group is now stretching up towards the twenty thousand square foot store and that the needs at this level are not the same as for smaller units. However, all sizes of units constitute our business and all can make good profits provided they are well managed.

We believe that our job as Group Wholesalers is to continue to supply the needs of our members and the services and advice necessary for continued development. This we will continue to do on a steadily increasing scale and we look forward to even fuller co-operation and support from you in the year ahead so that we may get in on the market.

Points of Interest

It is of interest to note that many of these changes have since occurred here in Ireland. For instance, in Dayton Ohio we visited National Cash Registers and it is interesting to note that at their sem-inar we discussed how they were developing what is now known as the "Scanning" system which today, 20 years later, is becoming standard practice here.

I also made a list of the many points of interest. The Statue of Liberty is on a small island and made of bronze that had now gone green. As it is hollow it is climbed by means of spiral stairs to her head, but was very wobbly. There were service cards in the hotel bedroom so that you could outline any complaints, this was then signed by the maid. Ticket display–holders were displayed in electric double decker trains – the inspector did not wait until you produced your ticket. The pedestrian crossing control lights said "Don't Walk" and "Walk". Iced water was served at all meals and coffee was served at every meal from beginning to end. Little was built to last – policy is to replace with more modern models every so often. Most cars were very big with eight cylinders, electric windows, power steering and servo assisted brakes. Motorways and fly-overs were everywhere. Cigars were cheap by our standards and mass produced goods were cheap too – shirts @ $3.50, ties @ $1.50, shoes @ $6.10, but very expensive if you wanted to be different or exclusive. The people were friendly, but could be abrupt or curt, especially if you wanted to upset their routine. They could be exceptionally generous too – many knew hard times. Things are well organised and people accept this, if one doesn't then one is told. The Irish were well accepted and there was a big "Irish" population in the East and the Mid West. Service at top county golf clubs is exceptional – shoes cleaned as soon as one took them off, but the annual subscription is $1,500! Soap and towels in the hotel were replaced every day, the glasses wrapped and there was colour television. Netball was the most popular spectator sport. Cities were divided into equal squares by the streets running north to south and east to west. One street was selected as 0 running in each direction and thus the next was 100, 200, 300 and so on in north or south and east and west of 0. Most public playgrounds we saw in Chicago were occupied by black and coloured children. Most workmen had the name of their company on the back of their jackets. Tipping is universal and usually 10% - 15%, it was not added at it was done at home. Book matches were free everywhere – hotels, restaurants, clubs etc. You need a car in Los Angeles as the "city" is 60 miles long and 35 miles wide; in fact, five areas are connected by freeways with four lanes each direction and a speed limit of 60 mph. The best money making game was selling postage stamps by a machine stating 25c – you put in 25c and get one 20c stamp. Americans are right, they don't believe in working for nothing! As you rise and fall according to results tension is high – so are ulcers!!

Personally, I found America to be fascinating and stimulating but quickly learned that one had to fight one's corner or be lost.

Between business calls we managed a tourist's trip of the sights of New York, visiting and climbing the Statue of Liberty, seeing China Town and Manhattan and going by lift to the top of the Empire State Building and visiting the United Nations. I also had a call from my cousin, Ruth Carter, whom I had never met. She invited us to her home in Chatham, New Jersey. The train that took us seemed straight from the Wild West. It was falling to pieces, packed full with passengers and the bar – believe it or not – consisted of a few rough planks thrown across some seats. This was one of the railways that surely was on the way out.

Few stations had names on them, but we did reach Chatham and then could not find her car that she had described as being "golden". While waiting in the railway station we had plenty of time to read all the notices about wanted felons, rapists, robbers and drug pushers. This was the other side of the USA.

Soon the gold car pulled up and I met my cousin and introduced Hugh and then off we were whisked to her flat. One of the first things I was asked was if I could mix a "Manhattan" and I could. Soon her son Bob and his wife Nancy arrived and then her daughter Lois and son-in-law Ralph Kitson, so the party got into full gear. Unfortunately, her other son Bill could not attend. We had a delightful evening and were invited out for dinner and we did not arrive back in New York until the small hours. Ruth was a charming, refined lady whose late husband was an official in the financial section of the White House. Her family seemed all very nice people so I was delighted that we had the opportunity to meet. She took an immediate liking to and admiration for Hugh and never failed to enquire for him in our correspondence up until the time of her death.

It's A Small Small World

We moved on to Dayton Ohio on the Saturday and introduced ourselves at National Cash Registers headquarters. They had been most helpful to me in organising our visit and we stayed there on a three day introductory course to American business which was most useful. One of their executives had a good Irish name of O'Sullivan and he invited us to see a bit of the countryside on the Sunday. He took us for a drive through the "blue grass" country of Kentucky. I was surprised to see the old style Georgian mansions with a rocking chair out on the porch. I thought that these had long since disappeared, but there they were just as in the movies.

We visited a stud farm and were shown around by a young black man. He showed us one of their top stallions and asked if we would like to buy. "He will only cost you a million dollars," he drawled with a big wide grin on his face. Next he said, "Where do you guys come from?" We answered "Ireland", and he queried "Dublin?"."No, from Cork," we said. "Well then you must know Ben Dunne!" he replied and we were knocked for six. Here we were thousands of miles from Cork and it was assumed that we must know this celebrity. The explanation was simple, as Ben had done business and kept some horses at the stud.

Our host was most helpful and when he heard that we wanted contacts in Los Angeles he said to leave it to him as his home was there and as he would be going home on the 30th he would arrange everything. On our last evening in Dayton all participants attended a farewell dinner at a well-known local restaurant. This was all self-service, but self-service at its very best. I never was faced with such a selection before or since. There was a huge range of starters; as big a range of soups; all kinds of fish including lobster, crab and salmon; an overwhelming selection of meats; and deserts and sweets to titillate the most discerning palate.

The proprietor was of Irish extraction and, on learning that two Irish were present, he was intent on being brought up-to-date and kept Hugh and me talking and drinking until the small hours. He presented each of us with a bottle of Bourbon and ordered a taxi to transfer us to our hotel – just because we were Irish! He had the only automatic bar that I have ever seen. A big variety of popular brands of spirits and beers were all connected to the long console and you simply applied the glass to the right tap and out came the appropriate measure. It was also computerised so you had complete stock control, sales analysis and re-order information.

Next we pushed on to Chicago – a beautiful city on the southwestern end of Lake Michigan, but the cold winds sweeping down from the Arctic would penetrate right through you. I had come some way prepared, but had to insist that Hugh visited a men's outfitters to buy a warmer outfit as I feared he may get pneumonia.

Once more I found myself having to fight my corner. On phoning our first contact, another Mr O'Sullivan, he said, "I am sorry, but I am afraid that I cannot see you today as I am in the middle of arranging a conference for several thousand delegated in Texas." I answered quickly, "Well, Mr O'Sullivan, that must be a huge job, but we have come as many miles to see you, so could you not spare us just an hour?". "Well," he replied, "I guess you have a point and, as you are Irish anyway, come and see my secretary and we will do our best."

Not alone did he give us an hour, but he gave us several most useful contacts, stood us lunch at his club, which was famous because it was here that during the great fire of 1871 that destroyed most of the city that businessmen continued to dine quite unperturbed. He then asked us to come back to his office when we had finished as he wanted to bring us home to meet his wife and family.

On the way to his lovely home in the suburbs we drove along Lake Shore Drive and he explained the ingenious method of traffic control. We had a fantastic evening and enjoyed a splendid meal with his charming wife and family. On hearing Hugh was a golfing enthusiast and anxious to get a game, he contacted a friend and arranged that on Sunday we would travel out on the electric railway to a nearby station. Here we would be met and brought to the golfing friend's office, as he would be working for a while.

The golf club was sumptuous. Locker rooms deeply carpeted, you left your shoes out and they were all polished up on your return. Once more American hospitality was unbelievable as we were invited to dinner. Coming back to Chicago, we arrived at an empty station as it was quite late. As we walked along the platform it was obvious that we were being followed. It was a most unpleasant feeling and we were glad to emerge on the street. We both felt that had we been alone we would surely have been mugged.

It was in Chicago that we learned much about Voluntary Group Trading. Their detailed services provided for the correct operation of each department through financial counselling, profit and loss analysis and so on. We also learned about a method called "Central Billing" which was to prove invaluable and now constitutes a very large part of our business. When I joined the company we had an arrangement called "Second Address" – whereby our representative took the order and this was then passed to the manufacturer and delivered directly. The manufacturer invoiced us and we invoiced our customer after adding a small profit. The difference with Central Billing is that not alone does the manufacturer supply directly at the retailer's request, but the wholesaler pays the manufacturer for a whole selection of orders with just one cheque. Furthermore, the price is an arranged price, governed by the size of the total business and the wholesaler passed this low price onto the retailer. His profit is a small discount at year end.

From Chicago we moved to Minneapolis in Minnesota – a charming city – and here we visited SuperValu and we were much fascinated by their showpiece, a fully carpeted supermarket with oak fittings and home style lighting, the concept being to make shopping as homely and pleasurable as possible. It was a truly magnificent store and they operated a unique system that I have never seen copied. Having completed and paid for your shopping you gave the number and location of your car and received a ticket and usually went to the beautiful restaurant. On leaving, you presented your ticket and your goods were delivered to the car – service with a capital S.

Then it was on to sprawling Los Angeles and our good friend from N.C.R. in Dayton had a car to meet us. The driver explained that he was at our disposal and had arranged to show us the sights the next day and this he did. We saw Hollywood, Beverly Hills, the famous wharf complete with old time sailing ships that function in so many movies and we saw a lot of Los Angeles. The sights the next day were much different as we were deposited at the door of Certified Grocers of California who occupied a site of seventeen acres, so big that it was hard to take it all in. This company provided practically everything for its customers and in their Fresh Fruit and Garden Produce section they had an innovation I had not seen elsewhere though I believe it is here now, i.e. artificial showers of rain at regular intervals to keep produce fresh.

On our last day we were picked up at 7.00 am for a visit to Disneyland and all its wonders. Our host provided the tickets for entrance to all the attractions and met us for lunch at the club – the only place in Disneyland that you can get a "real" drink. There we were joined by his lovely wife and later whisked off to their luxurious home to be introduced to their seven children, all with Irish names. To really finish off the day we were entertained to dinner and a nightclub – where could you match such hospitality.

The next day we flew over the Pole to London and home to Cork – it took us quite a while to get rid of our jet lag, but we brought back a wealth of information that started us off into General Merchandise, Central Billing and the aim of much higher standards of service for our retailers and the public.

While we were in the USA, Hugh learned that his much loved grandmother, the late John L. Musgrave's wife had passed away. She was a lovely person, gracious and quite unpretentious and he was sad and sorry that he was not at home when it happened. We also learned of the tragic sudden death of Desmond Eakins, Cash & Carry Manager, a very popular and much respected member of our staff. Desmond's son, John, today manages the Computer Department for scanning in SuperValu shops (the successor to VG).

Gladys and I also had another grandson. David Alexander McAfee was born on 15 July 1971.

CHAPTER 15

CHANGING TIMES AND A CHANGED NAME

We were now entering a new and greatly changed era, voluntary group trading and self-service were part and parcel of everyday life. Many manufacturers were co-operating very well, there was no problem in organising good promotions every fourteen days backed up with hand-bills and window-bills, there was regular advertising on television and in the press, smaller packs had been introduced and selling directly to retailers greatly curtailed. There were a few big manufacturers, notably Lever Brothers and Proctor & Gamble, Colgate Palmolive and the big confectionery manufacturers Fry Cadbury and Rowntree Mackintosh who still pursued the old bad habits. We continued to fight our corner and many battle royal was fought, but usually with mutual respect.

I will always recollect a very tough session with one of the above which continued over lunch and which erupted into a duel between the Managing Director and myself, with no contributions from the two teams listening in fascination to the play of words. Finally, my opponent lost his cool, "Mr Creighton," he almost bellowed, "You are just like Hitler!" Saying not one word I pulled a lock of my hair down across my forehead. For a moment there was dead silence and then we all broke into laughter.

To mark the changing times the Board decided that it was fitting to change the name of the company from Musgrave Brothers to Musgrave Limited. However, it took quite some time before people forgot the "Brothers" part, however most people just referred to the company as "Musgraves" – and they still do!

Another big change also occurred when the decision was taken to get out of the tea making/distributing business in which we had been involved for 96 years, relinquishing our interest to Brooke

THE LIFE AND TIMES OF ARTHUR HENRY   CHAPTER 15

Bond Liebig and Albright & Wilson Ireland Ltd. These formed a new company called Brooke Bond Oxo Ireland Ltd. This disposal was inevitable for, as we developed our group trading, we came into direct conflict with the national supermarket chains who were not disposed to support sales of tea connected with Musgrave through any of their outlets. This was a frightful drawback to our tea business. As mentioned previously, we also sold off our interest in the building company, Creative Stores Construction, to its Managing Director, Carl Campbell.

It is worth noting that our Managing Director, Hugh Mackeown, said at the year end review, "For your company, 1973 has been one of the most successful years in its history. Although we have undertaken nothing major in the way of new premises or diversifications, business has expanded as never before. The Irish economy as a whole has been doing well and we have been well placed to take advantage of this, especially through our great sales of general merchandise. In this context I am sure you would like me to mention also our Cash & Carry in Dublin which was opened 15 months ago and has consistently topped even our most optimistic forecasts ever since."

The man who spoke these words had already decided that in 1974 things would be entirely different in the matter of further development and new premises, although I do not think he thought that it would earn him the title of "Cash & Carry King". It was quite a spectacular decision to open three great Cash & Carry warehouses all in one year. However, it is necessary to understand the psychology behind the action.

Wholesale trade had suddenly woken up to the marvellous new method of doing business. With high inflation and rising distribution costs the concept of Cash & Carry was ideal. It was a low cost, low labour intensive operation. It is a cash business with the attraction of cash flow and it is a very welcome sight to see customers drive up to collect a van load of goods, pay cash and drive away. Musgrave plans were as follows:

164

CORK
The existing 16,000 square foot Cash & Carry in Cornmarket
Street in the centre of Cork was to be closed and a huge 120,000
foot Cash & Carry / warehouse complex to be opened. This
would also include Smiths Stores Limited – the Musgrave catering
division and there would be a warehouse and modern office
facilities in the development which would have a restaurant for
customers and parking for 350 cars. This will be built at
Ballycurren, on the Airport Road and is part of the major development plans for new Cash & Carry centres in Dublin and
Limerick as well, involving capital investment of £2·75 million

LIMERICK
Musgrave applied for planning permission for a 70,000 square
foot complex to be situated at Park on the main Dublin/ Limerick
Road. This would replace the 16,000 square foot Cash and Carry
at Mungret that has been trading in Limerick for the last five
years.

DUBLIN
Another spectacular one: 120,000 square foot complex was
scheduled for the north side of the city.This was to be situated at
Ballymun and the aim is to do on the north side of Dublin what
has been done at Robinhood on the southside.

At Tramore Road in Cork we were also involved in a major operation which was aptly called "Action '74". Our group consisted of
165 VG Supermarkets and 80 Shoprite Self-Service Convenience
style Stores. Our territory consisted of the province of Munster and
Laois, Kilkenny, Carlow and Wexford, and was divided into two
areas: East – under the control of Seamus Scally and West – under
the control of Terence Murphy.

Some of our more progressive members had expanded up to the
2,000 square foot range. Our overall average for VG was 7-800
square feet and for Shoprite 3-400 square feet. Whilst by and large

our VG operators were good in standards of hygiene and general appearance, they lacked uniformity and some were much better than others. We decided to do something to rectify this and devised a plan whereby all 165 supermarkets would get a visit from a team of merchandisers at a time agreed by the retailer and the area manager. The team would reorganise the whole supermarket, the object being to make it cleaner, brighter and more attractive and pleasant to shop in. Seamus and Terence were certainly kept busy and all the team put great heart and effort into the operation and it was a great success resulting in greatly increased sales that reflected in a much busier warehouse at Tramore Road.

We still had a certain amount of business with retailers who preferred to trade in the old fashioned or traditional manner, but more and more of the larger retailers had little time for "travellers".

I had noticed this trend and had reorganised accordingly, creating a new type of executive called a "consultant". These were very experienced men in self-service retailing drawn from the supermarket management section and their job was to see to it that all retailers were up to top standards in hygiene, layout, merchandising and overall profitability. It was common sense that our own profitability lay in our retailers profitability as we were, to all intents and purposes, one unit.

Our larger members were now not only into provisions and general merchandise but also fresh meat and, in this latter area especially, needed assistance in controlling this area professionally. We had two such men at that time – Jim Donovan and Bertie MacSweeney – and four commercial travellers – Bill Scriven, Gus Aherne, Tom Smyth and Con Carroll.

Con Carroll was a great character, an original "Knight of the Road" and he often kept us amused about his adventures. I recollect one he loved to tell. One of his toughest customers had a visit from a fast selling salesman for a cash register. Normally he would only allow such a man a brief few minutes as he hated slick salesman, but when he heard the misfortunate mention that he would give twenty-five pounds for the old cash register, a gleam came into his eye. "Twenty-five pounds did you say?" he asked. "Yes, twenty-five pounds, no matter what condition," was the reply. Reaching behind him he produced a well-worn biscuit tin and banging it on the counter said, "I'll take you on on that – here is my old register."

There was one further big event – Gladys and I were presented with another grandson and this time a Creighton, with the birth on 26 April, 1973 of Peter Byron.

Wise Management, Happy Staff

John Smith was now in charge of the warehouse and was very complimentary of its various departments. Of the buying department he said that Noel Hanly continued to run the department in a most successful way, assisted by Jim Trinder, and had now the added task of purchasing wines for our new wine department. Dermot O'Donoghue he congratulated for running the general merchandise department and also Mary Mullins, his very efficient secretary, without whose help he could not preform so well. In our computer section, we would be going direct early next year and he thanked John Eakins and also John Harris for his back-up stock-taking assistance. He spoke highly of John Kelleher who ran the very important despatch area and welcomed Tom Millard to the team. He also spoke of the great expertise of our forklift drivers especially Mattie Hurley and John Carroll; of Michael Barry, supervisor of the goods-inward section and the despatch office trio – Mary Hoare, Rose and Carmel Foley.

He also mentioned the transport department and the splendid drivers whom he said could not be beaten anywhere. These were Mick Hayes, John Bruton, Jack Hegarty, G. Buttimer, O. Gregory, Henry Cremin, John Cronin and J. Dempsey. Not to be forgotten, also the two ladies that ran the canteen, Mrs Nolan and Mrs Flood. John was a great organiser and leader and did a superb job of meshing the various functions to provide a smooth and efficient service, so vital to our operation, and he didn't forget to thank all concerned.

It is important to note that our retailers enumerated their requirements on the PLOF (price list order form) every week and posted this in, together with a cheque for the previous order to reach the warehouse at a specific time. Our deliveries also had to arrive at a specific time at their premises and all this entailed a very detailed synchronisation of operations.

The lads in the warehouse also had a soccer team competing regularly in the inter-firm competitions and during the winter months the Musgrave rings team kept the momentum going.

One of the big social events was the VG Charity Dance held annually, the proceeds of which were donated to a local charity. The organising of this literally started twelve months in advance – booking the ballroom and band and later organising sponsors for the spot prices and the dinner. The job was always in the very capable hands of Bill Kavanagh, assisted by Terence Murphy. Bill was a commercial traveller for many years and now specialised in advising retailers on how to increase profits by means of a careful mix of general merchandise.

We had great staff and Mary Hoare (who is now secretary to Pat Herlihy – Operations Director) summed it all up in verse:

Packages in, packages out
This is what life is all about;
With Jimmy and John we can't go wrong
Wrestling with problems all day long.
PLOFs of yellow, pink and buff
Make the going very rough.
When we think we're doing fine
We get a tinkle on the line –
Mrs "X"'s PLOF is late
And is just arriving at the gate!!
This makes us extra busy
And send us all in to a tizzy.

"Packs" fly left and "lines" fly right
And Carmel nearly dies of fright!
Miss Wiseman comes and goes all day,
Taking the PLOFs from Carmel's tray -
Keeping all the girls at bay
That's how Pricers earn their pay!

In the Packing Department 'tis "Murders" task
To fill the bins as fast as he's asked,
While the girls keep packing and wrapping all day
To ensure that they add "45" to their pay.
The "Goods-in" team are so busy counting
While the daily intake keeps on mounting.
Combies assembled and greased by Tom,
Insisting that the work goes on.

Forklift men, you will agree
Are a dashing lot for all to see:
John had been champion many a time –
His movements flow as though in rhyme.
And when you feel the day is long,
Mattie bursts out with a happy song.
Shampoos and toiletries are Derry's lot –
He's extremely happy with what he's got.
A soccer star, who can play the game,
Must some day bring our Michael fame.
And that makes up our Forklift Four –
The best in Ireland I'm very sure!

Next to come are the "Bulkers" eight
Who, from aisle to aisle, never hesitate:
"Skipped line", of course, are their mortal foe,
And if not done right, there's a tale of woe:
But "Plus 50" Bonus spurs them all,

And Tom is at their beck and call.
Putting up hardware is not like a dream,
But Conor and Bernard are a first-class team –
Everything from a pin to a pan,
The hardware Picker's "The Indispensable Man"!

Packages loaded and on their way
Enables our drivers to earn their pay.
Breakdowns make our Peter shake
Especially with so much at stake:
The garage staff he does inform
And asks them to undo the "harm":
And when at last repairs are done,
Mr Aherne's day has just begun.
To Rose come queries by the score
And, just when dealt with, along come more.
Warehouse wages are next in line –
Mr Walley say "They must be on time!"
And "Blondie" ringing on the phone
Makes our Mary feel like going home!
And when at last all jobs are done –
Mr. Smith agrees it was no fun.

About Secretaries and All That

Bruce Carswell now handed over the management of IMD (Central Office) to Tim Nolan and joined Musgrave's Main Board as Director in charge of General Merchandise Buying. Frank Walley was also appointed Accountant for our new Cash & Carry at Ballycurreen, Cork.

Needless to say, I was a very, very busy man, but I was very fortunate in always having a good secretary to keep my business affairs and my office functioning smoothly. My first was Pearl Kelleher, who was very efficient and an excellent typist, but Pearl left to get married. She was followed, in 1962, by Vivienne MacSweeney who was very vivacious and very efficient. Vivienne married Doctor Jackie O'Sullivan and went to live in Jersey. So, in 1964, I engaged Mary Cogan. Mary kept up the high standards of her predecessors while she stayed with us until 1968 when she also left to get married. I then engaged Mary Ruddy, who invited Gladys and me to her wedding and then departed to South Africa in 1970.

In May 1971, I selected a young lady from the sales office called Norma Roche who had joined us a year earlier. Unlike the others, she confessed that her typing was rusty and so was her shorthand. Nevertheless, I felt that this girl had a good brain and was a good worker and if I could succeed in training her to my way of doing things, so much the better. Poor Norma had a hard time and nearly packed it in, but we both persevered and soon she was a real treasure – a first-class secretary. On 4 January 1975 she was going to marry Dominic O'Sullivan, but she was staying in her job!

Now, with two children, Norma is personal assistant to Seamus Scally, Managing Director of SuperValu-Centra Distribution and Norma's husband is a sub-editor with *The Cork Examiner.*

CHAPTER 16

TIME IS MOVING ON

I was now 63 years of age and retirement loomed ever nearer, but I was so involved in a never ending succession of events that I hardly thought about it at all.

A big international event was planned by the VeGe Union to be held in the Congress Centre in Amsterdam on 16 - 18 March 1975. The Union was the central office for the VeGe organisation, operating in eleven European countries and organised these events with the last one being in 1935 celebrating its 25 year anniversary. We had a party of 21 arranged from Ireland, both North and South, and flew out from Dublin on the Sunday via London. Transfer time was very tight for our plane to Amsterdam and I led the way as I knew the airport well. I told all to follow me and all did – except three, who got lost, missed the flight and nearly ended up in Frankfurt. Fortunately they got to Amsterdam in time for the start of the celebrations.

This was to be my last such event and was special also for another reason, as this time Gladys accompanied me. What I did not know was that there was to be a third reason as you will see. We were sitting down to dinner in our hotel when we were informed that the candle-lit boat trip along the canal was about to begin, but the undoubtedly Irish waitress with her broad Kerry accent said that they would keep the meal hot for us. The boat trip was a great success and we were amply provided for with what we were told was Dutch wine! Be that as it may, it certainly worked wonders with our vocal cords and an uproarious sing-song soon was under way. By the time we finally got our dinner, duly kept hot, some of us – the more sensible ones – were ready for bed and we learned later that some eventually got to bed with the dawn!

The next morning the congress began in the magnificent centre. The main auditorium was vast and comfortably seated all one thousand six hundred delegates from eleven countries and we were welcomed by the rousing music provided by a splendid police brass band. Ceremonies began at ten o'clock and on the right armrest of each seat was a set of earphones, with channel indicators, volume control and an interpretation in six languages.

The inaugural address was by Mr D. C. Sipkes – Chairman VeGe Netherlands. He spoke of the history of VeGe trading and illustrated how it had adapted to changing systems, how it was still a very viable system and how it would always be functional, despite the introduction of hypermarkets and shopping centres. Other speakers were Mr Jean Rey, Minister of State for Belgium – Ex-Chairman of EEC, Doctor Omar Giame – Minister to the Republic of Somalia and Mr Carlo Troyan – Adviser of the EEC Commission of Agriculture.

The theme was collaboration between the developing countries and Europe and the needs of the Third World. In the lunch break we got an opportunity to visit the vast ranging food and drinks exhibition, held in the same building, which was mind boggling due the vast variety of goods on display. As there were all sorts of samples available we were in good form for our lunch that was served to perfection to all one thousand six hundred in the same auditorium. After lunch we were brought by bus to see the Hague and the village of Delpht where the world famous pottery of the same name is made. Gladys and I purchased a beautiful 37 centimetre wall plaque that now adorns our hall to remind us constantly of the wonderful times together.

That night we were invited by the Mayor of Amsterdam to a Holland Festival in the Hotel Krasnapolsky in the heart of Amsterdam. This was a fantastic event and a night never to be forgotten, or should I say – always to be remembered – depending on how your head felt the following morning. The festival area consisted of a large number of connecting rooms and there were innumerable eating places where, to begin with, a vast variety of starters were served consisting of various types of fish, cheeses, cold meats and fresh fruit. Of course, there was all the beer, spirits or wine that you wanted. In the evening there was a hot meal and as there were three different dance halls one found that a lot of refreshment, both solid and liquid, was needed as the night wore on. We has snake dances, Dutch dances, Irish dances and we had dances that nobody understood except for the dancers themselves! Everyone had a ball until the small hours.

During the evening Tim Nolan suggested that we get a breath of fresh air, so we went for a little walk but did not know exactly where we were going, just down the canal a little bit and over a bridge and where were we then – right in the middle of the red light district of Amsterdam and the temptations had to be seen to be believed.

Some of our party had never seen anything like this before and were amazed by it, especially by one window in which sat a voluptuous blonde wearing only a fan and Gladys, with a big grin and a nudge to one of them, said, "Why don't you go in Pat she would suit you fine". "For God's sake, Gladys," said Pat – aghast at such an idea. This was one outstanding business: on the ground floor was a nice restaurant, next floor beautiful and accommodating girls, top floor was blue films – what a world – we fled back to the festivities.

The following morning there was more hard work as the men returned to the conference hall where there were three presentations on representative examples of management with regard to the convenience store given by Mr A. Pandelitschka – Director of VeGe, Holland, Mr R. Foresi – Director of VeGe, Italy, and Mr R. A. Branston -Director of VG, England, successively. While we were hard at it, Gladys and the other ladies went on a tour to see the famous flower auction. She takes up the story here, "It was a fantastically large place, so large that participants went around on bicycles. Each buyer has his own seat, complete with computer terminal, facing a huge clock that had money amounts on the face rather then time numerals.

"Bidding was the reverse of what we practise at auctions here. The clock was set at the highest figure and moved to lower figures, when it reached what a buyer thought was his figure he pressed his button and the clock stopped, then that lot was his. The purchased lot was automatically transported down to the despatch area for packing and immediately despatched by air, which meant that flowers auctioned in the morning were on sale in places like London, Berlin and Paris within a few hours."

The ladies returned for lunch and in the afternoon one of the major events on the conference was staged. Each of the eleven countries had been asked to select a representative and this person was to be named "Mr VeGe". I did not know that I was to represent Ireland until Tim Nolan informed me, adding with a wry smile that he understood that a speech was required. I had little time, so I ran to my bedroom and, grabbing my piece of Hotel Alpha notepaper, I hastily concocted what I thought would be appropriate – although I had no idea what the ceremony would consist of. There was considerable difficulty in finding out and as there would be sixteen hundred people listening and looking, I felt that whatever it was it would have to be done right. The proceedings went like this:

Each country's name was called and that representative proceeded to the stage. First he was presented with a silver medallion, five centimetres in diameter, inscribed with the insignia "VeGe" in the centre, "Union International" on the surround and "Amsterdam 1975" was inscribed on the reverse, and also with a beautiful rose wood mallet with a silver mounting similarly inscribed. Symbolically this was to keep the manufacturers in control with a sharp blow from one side and to keep the retailer in check with similar treatment from the other. Quite a lovely token.

The representative then proceeded to the microphone where he gave a short address to those present, followed by congratulations and the presentation to Mr D.C. Sipkes – Chairman of VeGe, Netherlands and President of VeGe Union International. The countries represented were Austria, Belgium, Germany, Switzerland,

Spain, France, Great Britain, Ireland, Italy, Luxemburg, Netherlands. Here is what I said:

> Mr President, Ladies and Gentlemen, it is a very great pleasure for my colleagues from Ireland and for me also to be here in Amsterdam to participate in this wonderful congress.
>
> We are but a very small and young country on the fringe of Europe but we are very proud of our VG symbol. We are very proud to be part of the family of VeGe and to use your own picturesque speech of yesterday, we are very proud to have made history with you. We are fifteen years in VG and, particularly in our formative years, we were very much indebted and grateful for the wonderful help and encouragement we got from our friends in VeGe Holland, VeGe Germany, and from the inspiration and wonderful help we got from our very good friends in VG England. Now we like to think that the pupil is as good as the master!
>
> Some of us were also present at your twenty-five year anniversary, and each time we visit you do things better and better. Mr. President, we would like to congratulate you and VeGe International on a truly wonderful congress and to ask you to accept this small token as a souvenir of our visit.

There was a closing address by my friend Barry Gibson – Chairman of VeGe International and the ceremony closed with a sing-song. The whole proceedings were translated simultaneously into eight languages and received by the audience via headphones, but all was not over yet!

We learned that the adjoining exhibition was to be dismantled and that it was cheaper to give away the product than to transport them, so it was a case of "help yourself" – and we did. I saw one strong man stagger away with two dozen packs of canned beer slung over his shoulder, and he was Irish, but all in good spirits you could say. To round off the two day event there was a cocktail party in the Rijksmuseum (State museum) after which we were free to sample the delights of Amsterdam after dark. All I am going to say about that is that we were a very noisy lot when we returned to Hotel Alpha in the small hours. For me, I was very proud of my medallion and mallet and, although at the time it never entered my head, it was a fitting farewell to VeGe International and all the memorable visits my retailer colleagues and I had to Europe.

Two in a Row

For the company, 1975 was a year of huge expansion with the opening of our two new Cash & Carry warehouses in Limerick and Cork. The Limerick Park Road premises were opened by Counsellor Thady Coughlan – Mayor of Limerick. It was 85,000 square feet and cost three quarters of a million pounds.

Cork was even bigger, boasting 120,000 square feet and was opened by Jack Musgrave's wife, Molly, on 27 May. This complex also housed Smith's Stores who moved from their original premises in Camden Quay. The General Manager was Noel Murphy, the Accountant was Frank Walley and with the Managing Director, Hugh Mackeown, we had three men who had each represented Ireland in sport – Noel in rugby, Frank in athletics and Hugh in golf – quite unique.

The Directors present at the opening ceremony were, Hugh N. Mackeown, Hugh Musgrave (Stuart's son), Fred W. Markham, Patrick D. Hickey, John F. Smith, Ronnie Smith, Bruce Carwell and myself.

There was another unique event that took place also when our Chairman, Mr J. R. Musgrave, made a presentation to Mr Stuart Musgrave, the former Chairman, in recognition of 70 years of unbroken service with the company – surely an unbeatable record. Stuart Musgrave was a very fine gentleman and he and his lovely wife were near neighbours of ours when we lived in "Journey's End" and were considered one of Cork's most distinguished look-ing couples in earlier years.

Our business was also growing at Tramore Road, despite the harsher economic climate with growing unemployment now running at over one hundred thousand. We appointed a new Operations Manager to undertake the organisation of the warehouse and found the right man in Pat Herlihy. He was the former Sales Controller for the southern area with the Willwood Group. Pat is Operations Director today with the very capable assistance of Mary Hoare.

Always a believer in the old adage "Competition is the life of Trade" I had, for a number of years, organised a contest for our sales force, putting up the sum of £50 (quite good in money value then) for the representative whose trade would show the highest percentage increase at the end of the financial year. This kept the lads on their toes and, for reasons quite unknown, got the title of the "Local Derby". As we now had consultants as well as salesmen, I included them in the event with the same prize money for the area result. We continued to hold very informative annual conferences and these continue to this very day. It provided an opportunity to get all our retailers together, to get details of current and past performance in sales, new stores opened and expansions, and provided encouragement for individual endeavour in these areas.

We also looked at the year ahead, at new developments in trade, set our objectives and concluded with an open agenda of members' questions – this was often where the fireworks started. We also selected our local councillors and one of these chaired the meeting. It was a big event and we organised it to the last detail and finalised the day with a dinner and entertainment.

At this year's event I was complimented on my fine directing of operation and my selection as Mr VeGe at the International Congress in Amsterdam.

At the same meeting, compliments were also in order for Seamus Scally and Terence Murphy for their excellent performance in the field. We concentrated on bringing our members' skills into full focus, getting them to divulge the secrets of their success and outlining a blueprint for the year of our programme for the year ahead. This year the presenters were Mr Ken Brooks of Paisleys in Youghal and Mr Dan O'Mahony of Mallow.

In conjunction with manufacturers, we were continually organising competitions for consumers and painting competitions for children, all tied in with purchasers. I usually made a presentation of a bicycle, or whatever, to the winner in the local shop. This provided not alone stimulus to trade, but involved our retailers in their own community, providing valuable attachments.

Another important event must be recorded. Gladys and I became grandparents for the eighth and final time with the arrival of Andrew George Creighton on 26 February 1975.

CHAPTER 17

THE GRANDE FINALE

Musgrave Limited entered, in 1976, its centenary year in fine shape. Little could the two brothers, Thomas and Stuart, have envisaged that their modest beginnings one hundred years ago in North Main Street, Cork, would have grown into Ireland's leading distribution business, not by accident or good fortune, but by great leadership, sound judgement, solid business principles and the ability to activate a splendid work force – plus hard work by all.

Hugh Mackeown could report another year of good progress. Our Delivered Operation to VG Supermarkets had traded very well indeed and the three Cash and Carries were going great. Building had commenced on a new £2.5 million Cash & Carry at Ballymun in North Dublin, scheduled to come into operation in the Autumn of 1977. For many years the company had operated a long service award of a gold watch and it is interesting to record those who had qualified in our centenary year:

Sheila Barret	Matt Hurley	Kitty Wiseman
Josie Fahy	Billy Livingston	Maurice Coughlan
Molly Rasmussen	Jim Murphy	Joe Devlin
Kathleen Winning	Dan Sheehan	Mick Hayes
John Casey	Maureen Dolan	Christy Kingston
Arthur Creighton	Nancy Motherway	Willie Locke
John Harris	Bridie Taylor	Mick Murphy
	Eddie Wall	Jim Trinder

By now retirement was literally on my door with the announcement that, "As from 1 January 1977, Mr John F. Smith – Group Operation Director will assume full responsibility for the running of the Delivered division. Mr Seamus Scally, Group Marketing

Manager, will assume Mr Creighton's responsibilities leading up to his retirement in July of that year." Terence Murphy was appointed Area Sales Manager of the Eastern area and a new appointee, John McNamara, was to take over his former responsibilities in the Western area. Another appointment was that of Mitchel Barry as Marketing Director of Musgrave (Provisions) Ltd. Provisions was now distributing Ross Frozen Foods throughout the Republic – a very important agency. Another important man in the company was Brian Mahony, now Group Accountant, whose job was to collate the accounts from the Cash & Carries and Delivered Trade, add in overheads, income and expenditure and arrive at consolidated results for the management of Musgrave Group as a whole. Bill Kavanagh had been appointed General Merchandise Sales Manager. With the sale of our tea business to Brooke Bond Oxo, my brother, Bill, was transferred to Inwards Group Controller at Robinhood Cash & Carry, Dublin.

For my part, I was very pleased with the appointment of John Smith and Seamus Scally as the two men designated to carry on with the management and development of the project so dear to my heart – the two voluntary groups. John Smith was blessed with outstanding business ability and Seamus Scally had proved himself an excellent manager and organiser, with a wide and expansionist view of the retail food business.

I knew our group would need reorganisation on a large scale, especially in the VG area. Here we had developed into a mixture of supermarkets of quite large proportions and much smaller units, and each were more and more diverging. The big units were in direct competition with the multiples, their retail prices had to be keener, as had their special offers. They needed tighter controls and also needed to be further developed. Pat Hickey had discovered that the name "Super Valu" (a big chain in the USA) was not registered in Ireland and he had made it secure for Musgrave Ltd. We knew we had in our group some of the most progressive and expansion-minded independent retailers in Ireland but they needed leadership and special treatment. John Smith and Seamus Scally were the right men to undertake this huge job and lead our group on into the eighties and nineties. All would be well when I departed – I was happy.

Most Exciting – Very Entertaining But Sad!

As for now, another big event was in the offing – our English friends had organised a convention to celebrate 21 years and this was to be held on 26 October 1976, in the Nissaki Beach Hotel on the island of Corfu and would include a few extra days to celebrate. The total group was being drawn from England, Scotland, Northern Ireland, Wales and the Republic and amounted to three hundred and 84 delegates. Tim Nolan had organised a party of 22 from the Republic. Two 707 Boeing jets were chartered to transport us all from Gatwick Airport outside London. However, our journey was not without incident, as we had a long delay in Dublin and tremendous difficulty in locating the bus for Gatwick Airport when we arrived in Heathrow Airport – in fact, we thought we would not get there at all.

When we did get going our spirits were so high that we had a great sing-song on the way – it is hard to keep Irish spirits subdued for long! Gladys was with me again, as were my old friends John Riordan of Fermoy and his lovely wife Pru, John Joe Harold from Newcastle West, Jimmy Strappe and his wife Gertie from Golden Co. Tipperary, Joe and Ursula O'Leary from Limerick, Jack O'Shea and his charming wife Madeline from Cobh and Jack Keogh from Templemore, as well as a group from the Niland and Garvey areas.

Corfu is a wonderful green island, very mountainous with innumerable beaches and little harbours. Looking down from the air one would wonder where we could land but our pilot took us down in such a steep dive that we landed almost breathless, the single airstrip just long enough to accommodate a 707. The roads were literally stuck on to the mountainsides and consisted of continuous hairpin bends and as Gladys and I were in the back seat all we could see at times was the sheer drop into the sea or valley below! However, we are good travellers and quite enjoyed it all. The Nissaki Beach Hotel is a big luxury hotel sitting on the water's edge at the foot of a steep cliff and the access road is a marvel of judgement for any driver. The entrance is in the centre of the building with eight stories above and eight stories below to the beach. The main lounge accommodates four hundred with ease. There was an official reception by the Prefect of Corfu followed by a "Get-Together" dinner and dance – with Greek music, naturally.

The conference theme the next day was aptly named "Making Money – Using Money – Keeping Money" and was opened by Dick Branston, who spoke of 21 years of VG and the problems they had overcome, the prospects for the future, and he rightly emphasised the sound principles of the system.

"Making Money" was a very interesting presentation by Colm Sibbald, who ran a chain of twelve VG supermarkets in England. He demonstrated his own experience of running successful supermarkets and utilising profits to expand into more. He said he had tried buying directly from manufacturers, but the VG system had made him more money. We then had Mr Ken Webb – Chairman of Birds Eye, who demonstrated the skilful use of stock control, credit facilities and cash flow to maximise profits. Our last speaker was even more interesting, Mr Ken Davy – an investment and assurance consultant – who dealt with keeping money. This centred around the absolute necessity of better knowledge of the final points of taxation and he provided many examples bearing on capital gains tax, capital transfer tax, income tax and investment. Although English tax and Irish tax differ, we found it put us all thinking.

The following few days were so organised that we got a good look at the island. We found Corfu town to be a delightful blend of quaint narrow streets, some splendid public buildings, fine open squares and a delightful harbour.

We also found great excitement, great amusement and some consternation at the sight of Pat O'Shea and Madeline, hats askew, driving in great style, but in the wrong direction on a one-way street! The ladies loved the shops, nothing was priced and just as the Irish love to bargain, the Greeks were worthy opponents. The scenery was absolutely beautiful, mountains, fishing villages, sandy bays and sea views all blending into a fascinating kaleidoscope of colour and beauty. Life is old fashioned and there is a big divide between rich and poor. The island is densely covered with olive trees, some of which we were told could be up to two thousand years old. We men got one big eye opener – the women did most of the farm work while the men gossiped, smoked and sipped ouzo (a popular aniseed flavoured drink) – or so we were lead to believe. We certainly saw far more women than men picking olives.

Whoever organised the affair did a great job in transporting us to a wide variety of Tavernas, where the atmosphere and the food were so different. In one of these, huge platefuls of roast meat and vegetables were placed on enormous dishes on long, rough, timber tables and you helped yourself to as much food and drinks you could sustain. Another had two whole lambs roasting over a charcoal fire as we entered – the aroma was fantastic.

Every night we had Greek dancing, sometimes in the back yard and sometimes in the garden and we had wonderful sing-songs that went on into the small hours in various languages and dialects. It was great fun and on our last night we had a gala dinner and dance, preceded by a champagne reception. During the evening, a retirement presentation of a beautiful onyx trinket box, bound in gold and with gold feet was made to me by Tim Nolan on behalf of our group and there was a bouquet of flowers for Gladys – a delightful and much appreciated gesture and a perfect memento of my final conference with all my VG friends from the British Isles. It was a very interesting and enjoyable occasion and Cork seemed quite a dull place after it – but the work had to go on.

The Sweet Rewards for Success

We were now into 1977 and I was due to retire on my sixty-fifth birthday – 29 July – and was busy organising my run-down schedule and easing Seamus Scally into his new position. Sitting in my office on Monday 7 March, while engrossed in my work I was interrupted by Fred Markham who informed me that there had been a snap Board Meeting arranged and suggested that I go with him. I was a little puzzled at the urgency, but went along completely overlooking the significant date.

My fellow directors had remembered that it was exactly 50 years ago on that day that I had begun my career with Musgrave Ltd. I have never, to this day, found out who had the wonderful brainwave in selecting a suitable item to fit such an occasion, but it was brilliant. Jack Musgrave shook my hand and presented me with a solid silver rose bowl 126 years old – the age represented the combined number of years that the Creighton family had served the company. Also present were Hugh Mackeown – Managing Director, Hugh Musgrave – Vice Chairman, John Smith – Operations Director and Fred Markham – Financial Director. Jack said that in introducing and developing the VG system so successfully I had performed a signal service for the company and congratulated me on such a wonderful achievement of 50 years of dedication and hard work. I was quite overwhelmed but managed to express my thanks and said that I would always treasure that day in my memory as a very special day in my life. I quoted the late Sir Thomas Lipton's motto " There is no fun like work," and truthfully said how I thoroughly enjoyed it all.

Later in the week there was another presentation of a silver cruet given by Seamus Scally on behalf of the sales staff and still another, a fine Waterford Crystal vase, on behalf of the older members of the staff.

Those present were Bridie Taylor, Kathleen Winning, Kittie Wiseman, Josie Fahy, Nancy Motherway, Paddy Simpson, Dermot O'Donoghue, Noel Hanly, John Harris, Joe Devlin, John Eakins, Brian Mahony, John Donovan, Jim Trinder and Dan Sheehan, and the presentation made by Pat Herlihy.

To round off such an eventful week Gladys and I entertained the directors, sales department and older staff to a night out at the South County Bar in Douglas, an event greatly enjoyed and much appreciated by all. A very memorable occasion it turned out to be.

In the company magazine *Musgrave News*, Hugh Mackeown said that 100 years is a long time in the life of a company but, relatively speaking, 50 years is very much longer in the life of an individual. He was, of course, referring to me in so far as I had contributed to the growth of the company during half of its one hundred years. "When," he said, "we relate this span of time to the degree of expertise and dedication Arthur has brought to every undertaking, we can see how truly remarkable his achievement is."

My Final Trip

I had one more trip abroad before I retired – once again to the USA. This time Tim Nolan organised a visit and my companions were Hugh Mackeown, Michael Niland, Dan Griffen (also of Nilands), John Smith and Louis Garvey.

We first visited San Francisco – our objective to view the supermarkets' techniques. It was very interesting for Hugh and for me to compare this to our last visit and what it did bring home was the remarkable strides that had been made in Ireland in the intervening six years. We still had plenty to learn, especially in the massive merchandising displays and sheer size of variety of goods carried, but these latter points are not really relevant when you compare our tiny country with this giant.

We all liked San Francisco. It has great charm, almost "old world" in American terms. It is very hilly and the famous tram cars clatter up and down continuously. Here I saw my first exterior lift and also the marvel of the Portland Bridge, eight miles long and with two tiers of traffic – one running above the other. Personally, I was somewhat disappointed at the famous Golden Gate Bridge. It is a wonderful piece of engineering, but it is dull red in colour; perhaps it was the name that put me off as I expected something more glamourous. We also went to see the biggest trees in the world, the giant Sequoia or Redwood. These are unbelievable giants! They reach heights of over 300 feet and have a diameter of up to 36 feet with some being thousands of years old. Standing beside one of those really makes one feel quite small and insignificant – quite a humbling experience.

The high-rise buildings tend to make the streets appear narrow, but they carry four or six lanes of traffic. Many of the buildings rest on concrete and steel legs. One most unusual forty storey giant, with each storey diminishing in size, looks like the tallest church steeple you ever saw – but it is teaming with office workers. Another that we visited had a revolving restaurant on the top that enabled one to enjoy the continuously changing pattern of skyline. So good is the road network that Americans think nothing of commuting 60-80 miles to work each day. It was in San Francisco that we saw our first push-button automatic automobiles that are commonplace here now.

America is a nation made up of a mixture of most of the world's nationalities and these people tend to maintain their national cultures, languages, eating habits and their own localities. This has a direct bearing on the range of goods carried by supermarkets. Those in an Italian district would feature a wide selection of Italian foods, in a Chinese district there would be Chinese foods and so on. Some would cater for several different ethnic tastes.

The same applies to the restaurants and there is a Chinese district in San Francisco where we had a great experience of a full-size Chinese dinner – complete with chopsticks. That was fun and I think that John Smith won on his mastery of that art. We also dined at the famous Fisherman's Wharf where the smell of cooking fish prevails the atmosphere. The fish is wonderful as it is absolutely fresh. This is so important in food, for no matter what the pundits may say, any food after deep freezing tends to have its flavour and texture altered. There is nothing like fresh food!

Hugh Mackeown departed for Cork and Tim Nolan went to

Vancouver, Canada, to relive earlier memories. John, Louis, Dan, Michael and I decided to take a leisurely route home and see a little more of the USA. Our first stop was at the world famous Las Vegas in the middle of the Nevada desert. At the airport you are greeted with gaming machines, there is a numbers game in progress as you breakfast at MacDonalds. The vast gaming halls in Las Vegas have to be seen to be believed. Some are devoted to one-arm bandits, the big American silver dollar is common currency, and you are provided with a plastic bucket to hold your winnings. We met one lady who was going great on a winning streak and her bucket was half full.

Her husband urged her to stop then but was told, "I am winning wise guy, you get lost," she pulled the lever and received a cascade of coins. Later we passed her way again and, alas, the bucket was empty – Lady Luck is very fickle.

We spent a few days in Las Vegas and went to a fabulous stage show including a fantastic display of Cleopatra's entry into Rome – complete with live elephants, leopards, tigers, chained slaves and topless dancers. The finest shows world wide regularly performed in Las Vegas, there are also big boxing events and all sorts of all night entertainment going on non-stop. It certainly has to be seen to be fully comprehended.

Our flight to Miami was a leisurely affair and we touched down at Houston and Jacksonville. We were also provided with free champagne all the way. Needless to say we arrived in splendid order demonstrated fully by John Smith who insisted on getting into a vintage car that was on display and he blew the horn until our ears vibrated. Our taxi driver was a Puerto Rican and was fascinated by our peculiar accents (to him). He asked us where we came from and as we said we were from Cork in Ireland we got a reply that put us into peals of laughter. "Isn't that out Houston way?" The poor fellow had never even heard of Ireland, not to mind Cork.

We found Miami disappointing as we expected a place much more glamourous, but we enjoyed a visit to the Everglades with its fantastic parade of pleasure boats of all descriptions and we saw a man who made his living wrestling with alligators – what a vocation! However, we had a very enjoyable visit and Michael Niland and I, being in a similar age group, became very good friends.

Some More Changes

Back home, the run-down to my departure (on 5 July) had started to roll. I retired as Chairman of VG Services on 5 July 1977. We had a splendid party at the Goat Restaurant in Dublin and I was presented by Tim Nolan with an instant Kodak Camera and a mahogany nest of tables on behalf of the Board. Present were Jack Burke and Dan Griffin of Niland in Galway, Louis Garvey and Brendan Cassidy of Garvey's in Drogheda, Rex Coghlan and Frank Campbell of Central Office and John Smith.

Some further changes had also taken place at Musgrave Limited. In addition to John Smith now being Director in charge of Distribution and Seamus Scally as Marketing Manager, we had a new Buying Administrator Manager in Greg Cantillon.

His first and most important task was to develop the system of Central Billing that Hugh Mackeown and I had found operating so well in the USA. For some strange reason that I could never fathom, Jack Musgrave did not agree with me that this was a very important development that required a new full-time operator to develop. The system now constitutes a highly important part of our system and profits but we could have introduced it years earlier. Pat Herlihy was appointed Operations Manager and Frank Walley returned from the comforts of Airport Road as Chief Accountant of the distribution division. We also had a new store engineer responsible for the development of retailer supermarkets in Cyril Riordan, who graduated from Cork school of Building as an architectural technician and had considerable experience in Cork County Council. John Smith had his team together to develop our bigger retailers under the SuperValu symbol and the remainder of the group went under the Centra symbol. The VG and Shoprite symbols were subsequently withdrawn.

A Wonderful Way to Say Farewell

I retired on my birthday, 29 July 1977, and on the night of 2 August, a Tuesday following the bank holiday Monday, the directors had arranged a final send-off farewell dinner and dance at the Metropole Hotel. All our family were invited as special guests and there was a wide selection of retailers and their wives, our own staff from, not alone Tramore Road warehouse but also Cork and Limerick Cash & Carries and all the directors and their wives. Also there was Dan Griffin and Louis Garvey. It was a truly well represented occasion. My good friend Barry Collins from Carrigaline was in the Chair and, very wisely, decided to get the presentations over first so that all could then enjoy the rest of the evening uninterrupted.

On behalf of the retailers, John Riordan of Fermoy started the speeches. Having stressed the big contribution I had made to the Independent Trade he said that they were all very proud to have been associated with me in this development. "I suppose I can speak for many of us when I say that from time to time we had our differences with Arthur," he said, "he was tough and, God knows, he needed to be in dealing with some of us – but he was fair."

He referred to the great times we had in Europe together with me and Gladys and he wished us Bon Voyage and a happy retirement. We already knew that the retailers' farewell gift was a holiday of our choice anywhere in the world. Hugh Mackeown was next followed by Jack Musgrave and they both spoke of the difference group trading had made to Musgrave Limited. Jack remembered me quoting Confucius when we decided to introduce VG saying, "A journey of a thousand miles begins with the first step".

Dan Griffin said, "Nilands owed a perpetual debt of gratitude to Arthur for having introduced them to VG". This was followed by the presentation – first the holiday from the retailers plus a cheque for spending money and an inscribed silver tray, a fine Sanyo music centre, plus a generous cheque for records from the company. A magnificent once-off Galway crystal vase from Nilands, all of 35 millimetres tall and a delightful framed oil of Connemara by Marjoram from Garveys of Drogheda.

I was wondering what on earth I could say in reply. How is it that we reserve all the nice things to say about our fellow humans for when they are about to leave us? Whatever the reason, it certainly makes the object of the praise feel good and I felt very proud and quite overwhelmed by the enormous goodwill and friendliness.

In my speech, which I knew would be my last to my colleagues and retail friends, I said, "No words of mine could express my feeling at such a fantastic reception, such glowing tributes and magnificent presentations to me and my wife." I brought Gladys into it, as during all the years since I had the honour to introduce VG in 1960, she had been a tower of strength and inspiration – especially in the early days of up-hill struggle. I referred to the pioneering spirit of our start-up and the perpetual debt we owed our older members and I said we were delighted to have some of them with us. I thanked Jack for the opportunity he gave me and for his and Hugh's support and I paid tribute to the great team of workers I had behind me and I wished John and Seamus every success in the future. I then said, "I think the finest thing I got from Group Trading was not the deep sense of satisfaction, or the marvellous feeling of success, but the much more rewarding comradeship."

I also spoke about our visits to Europe and what deep satisfaction it gave me to see our businesses grow together. I thanked the directors and my colleagues in the company and central office in Dublin and said how I was delighted to see Nilands and Garveys and their retailers share in our success.

I thought that would be the end of it, but Barry Collins thought differently. He said that amongst other things, "I have one sad note to strike and I have a very special presentation for Gladys. I heard that poor old Arthur can't keep her warm in bed any longer and we all felt that we must do something about this, hence this special presentation of a dual control electric blanket which we are sure will solve all their problems." This produced roars of laughter and when it subsided he presented Gladys with an ornamental Cavan cut glass centre piece as a token of esteem from the retailers. Gladys thanked them and said she endorsed all I had said and that she was delighted and surprised at the most unexpected beautiful piece of cut glass, but, regarding the electric blanket she would deal with Barry later.

By now we were full up with speeches but badly in need of food and drink. The meal that followed was the very best the Metropole chefs could produce and was thoroughly enjoyed by all. Next it was time for dancing and meeting all our old friends. No party could be complete without a song or two and so all had to endure, amongst many renderings, my version of "Some Enchanted Evening" followed by the "Rose of Tralee". Barry's "Who Killed Cock Robin" brought down the house.

EPILOGUE

As I predicted, John Smith and Seamus Scally made a great success of introducing the Super Valu symbol for all the larger supermarkets in our Group and the Centra symbol for the smaller convenience style outfits. The VG and Shoprite symbols were withdrawn. There are now 142 Super Valu supermarkets spread out throughout the whole Republic of Ireland and 218 Centra stores, making us a fully national organisation. The distinctive monarch red and buttermilk colours of Super Valu Supermarkets and the equally distinctive midnight blue and buttermilk colours of Centra stores are easily recognisable and a distinctive feature of cities and town nationwide.

There are 66 founder members who still trade under the original family ownership, name and address – quite a remarkable signpost to the huge success of the system. Eleven members operate more than one supermarket. The Caulfield brothers run five supermarkets located at Bandon, Co. Cork, Ballybeg, Co. Longford, Callan, Co. Kilkenny, New Ross, Co. Wexford and in Tipperary Town.

My valued friend Thomas Garvey of Dingle operates in his home town and also in Tralee, Castleisland, Cashel and also has a thriving abattoir in Tralee. Thomas's late father Jim and his wife Kate traded with me very successfully when I was "on the road" and Gladys and I are life-long friends of the family. Little did I dream that the sturdy little boy who stood at his mother's side as she and I did business, taking a great interest in what was going on, would one day become such a successful entrepreneur. His mother Kate still lives in the original home just a few steps away from the supermarket. This is a strange and remarkable world and both she and I are surely blessed to still be around and able to derive such immense pleasure in the success of the system. A system introduced by Jack Musgrave and with his support put into motion by myself, with the

valued assistance of Willie MacBrateney, Pat Hickey and our coura-
geous retail friends.

Unfortunately, Jack is no longer with us as he passed away quite
suddenly in December 1984, to be followed by the death of John
Smith five years later in January 1989, both quite different but
remarkable gentlemen who are sadly missed by their families and
also by their colleagues and friends, but who each made an invaluable contribution to the success of Musgrave Ltd.

I had also lost my beloved brother Bill, who passed away on 14
November 1977, thus leaving my eldest brother Charles (nicknamed
Addie) and me – the only surviving members of our family.

Musgrave Limited is now the largest distribution company in the
Republic. In addition to the symbol groups, we have six super size
Cash & Carry warehouses situated at Robinhood Industrial Estate
and St Margaret's Road, Ballymun, and Sallynoggin, in Dublin; at
Tuam Road in Galway; Park Road in Limerick; Airport Road in Cork
and one at Duncrue Road outside Belfast and at Pennybarn
Industrial Estate Derry in Northern Ireland. The total turnover was
just short of £500 million at the end of our last financial year,
December 1993. The company now employs over 1000 people and
taking into consideration the thousands employed by, not alone our
group retailers in their own businesses, but, by the 20,000 trade
customers on our Cash & Carry books, our distribution business is a
very substantial player in the economy of this country.

As for Gladys and me, following on from that splendid farewell
party way back in 1977, we now faced a whole new way of life.
Volumes have been written about how to cope with retirement but I
must say we adjusted very smoothly and enjoyably.

Our attitude to life has always been "do not wait for things to
happen but get in there and make things happen" and "Get all the
fun, excitement and satisfaction you can from every day".

We sold Rochestown House in 1978 and once again, using
Gladys's formula of trading down as the family gets smaller – we
did very nicely in the process. We now live in a very comfortable

bungalow situated to get as much sunshine as possible, in the same area of Rochestown. We are fortunate in our common love of gardening and it is our main preoccupation. We produce all our bedding plants from seed and have over one hundred roses and a carefully chosen selection of shrubs to provide colour and delight all year long. I grow most of our vegetable needs, again from seed, and very often complete the full cycle by making soups and pickles and freezing. Indeed, I quite enjoy a bit of cooking also and do all our maintenance work and also a little writing.

We love the outside world and enjoy walking, especially by the sea. Between these activities and two holidays abroad each year, life is very rewarding. We are both octogenarians, but don't tell anyone, 'cause otherwise you'd never know ...